Essentials of Public Opinion

Bernard Hennessy
California State University
Hayward

With the assistance of
Erna Hennessy

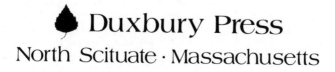 Duxbury Press

North Scituate · Massachusetts

The cover print, "The Verdict of the People," by George Caleb Bingham (1811-1879) is from the collection of the Boatmen's National Bank of St. Louis.

Besides being probably America's best known frontier painter of the nineteenth century, Bingham was a politician from a family of politicians. He was a member of the Missouri State Legislature from 1848 to 1853, was State Treasurer from 1862 to 1865, and was twice a candidate for Congress (1866 and 1874). "The Verdict of the People" was completed in 1855.

Duxbury Press

A DIVISION OF WADSWORTH PUBLISHING COMPANY, INC.

Essentials of Public Opinion was edited and prepared for composition by Katharine Tsioulcas. Interior design was provided by Sandy Levitz.

L.C. Cat. Card No.: 75-11272
ISBN 0-87872-097-9

PRINTED IN THE UNITED STATES OF AMERICA

1 2 3 4 5 6 7 8 9 10 – 79 78 77 76 75

Contents

Preface

This is, generally, a condensed version of my larger text, *Public Opinion* (third edition 1975). That was written for a one-quarter or one-semester upper-division course in public opinion. This excerpted version has been created as a supplement for introductory American politics courses or for the course that combines public opinion with parties, or pressure groups, or political behavior, and in which instructors prefer to use several shorter and less expensive texts. Much of the larger book has, of course, been omitted in this. The materials kept and the new materials added have been reorganized into seven chapters that are, I hope, conceptual, analytical, and behavioral. Some instructors, inevitably, will disagree with what I think to be the "essentials" of public opinion, preferring more of this or less of that or something entirely different. I hope, however, that I deal with this vast and vexing subject in at least enough detail so the student, in the end, will know why I say it is vast and vexing. Footnotes may lead on those who are curious or serious or both.

One stylistic feature of this book needs commenting on. For some time I have been concerned about English language sexism. While not militant about anything nowadays, I am a feminist, and want to help overcome those social and cultural traits that impoverish all of us by discriminating against half of us. Our language habits are among the worst of our sexist cultural patterns; they insidiously suggest that the male pronouns are the proper and normal ones and the female pronouns are to be used only in secondary and deviant cases. A person is always a he unless we are pointing to a particular she.

However, to observe the pervasiveness, and the implied inequity, is only to recognize the problem. The remedy, after so many hundreds of years, is neither obvious nor easy. Shall we use circumlocutions for words like *mankind*, and say "the two-legged animal?" Shall we create neologisms and substitute "chairperson" for *chairman*? Shall we use indirection, plural forms, and the passive voice to get rid of the generic "hes" and "hims" that convention has long approved? In experimentation I have tried all these stratagems, and have found them all unsatisfactory.

So, in this book I adopted another device — which is also unsatisfactory. But it has the advantage over the other devices of being noticeable, even jarring. I have simply assumed an equality of the sexes in talking about generic and exemplary persons. Sometimes the voter is referred to as he and sometimes as she. Sometimes the political leader is re-elected in her district and sometimes in his district. I think it would be useful if we who are the temporary custodians of the English language developed new sexless nouns and pronouns. I hope my unorthodoxy in this book will both draw attention to the subtle sexism of our prose and hurry its disappearance.

I am grateful to Joe Bindley of Wittenberg University, Steven Chaffee of the University of Wisconsin, Reo Christenson of Miami University, Don Freeman of the University of West Florida, Jerry Kline of the University of Michigan, and Samuel "Pat" Patterson of the University of Iowa. They made me work a little harder. But their suggestions were good ones and improved both the content and clarity of this book.

I am also grateful to Bob Gormley, Duxbury Publisher. I wanted to call this book "Less on Public Opinion" and rename the larger text "More on Public Opinion." Gormley talked me out of that. He said I couldn't even mention it in the Preface.

BERNARD HENNESSY

1 Opinions and Democracy

We start, quite simply, with a definition: Public opinion is the complex of preferences expressed by a significant number of people on an issue of general importance.

That is a dry and academic definition that I will try to show to be more useful than other definitions that might be offered by politicians or journalists. Whatever public opinion is, a lot of people have thought about it for a long time. Vox populi, the voice of the people, to the Romans had special meaning – a meaning carried on and down the centuries by the democrats of the modern world.

Rousseau is sometimes said to have been the first modern political thinker to make an extended analysis of public opinion. He appreciated that opinions have their origin not in nature or in supernatural powers, but in social relationships. He was aware that all governments rest fundamentally on opinion rather than on law or coercion, and that in social change no government may be very far ahead of popular acceptance. He knew, too, that governments make opinions as well as reflect it: "It is certain," he said, "that all peoples become in the long run what the government makes them: warriors, citizens, men, when it so pleases; or merely populace and rabble, when it chooses to make them so."[1]

As a social and political phenomenon, public opinion was of little concern to the holders of power before the ideological revolution of the eighteenth century. It was quite clear that the effect of the equalitarian and majoritarian ideas of Locke, Rousseau, Condorcet, Jefferson, and the other thinkers of the period 1650-1800 was to widen the base of political power. Prior to this period it did not matter much what the public thought — the public had no way to make its opinions either known or effective in determining policy. But the emphasis on political equality and individualism, coupled with the perhaps more important technological and economic changes of the eighteenth century, meant that a growing part of the hitherto voiceless public would be able to influence governmental policy; and when the public begins to influence policy, it becomes important what the public thinks. Thus, by the opening of the nineteenth century, the term *public opinion* had gained a fairly wide usage among the educated classes.

How one defines public opinion depends partly on what one thinks of it. In 1820 the British statesman Sir Robert Peel thought poorly of, as he put it, "that great compound of folly, weakness, prejudice, wrong feeling, right feeling, obstinacy, and newspaper paragraphs, which is called public opinion." One hundred years later an American political scientist, Edward Sait, tried to convince his academic readers that "there should be no question about what we mean by calling opinion 'public'; we mean, in the light of long-established usage, the opinion of the people, the opinion of the community"; he had no patience with "sociologists and psychologists [who], without the support of any previous authority, have tried to substitute a meaning of their own."[2]

But those whom Sait called "unsupported" sociologists and psychologists were searching for greater precision of definition — they wanted to know *what* public and *what* opinion, and *what difference it makes, to whom, and when.*

It may be of some value to examine our definition by looking more carefully at its basic elements — at what might be called the *factors* of public opinion. There appear to be five such factors in most of the recent attempts to define public opinion.

1 Presence of an Issue. There is, in the first place, a virtual consensus that public opinion gathers around an issue.

In common use *public opinion* often appears to be a generalized term, describing something like a collective attitude or a public mood. People often say, for instance, that everyone should respect public opinion, that public opinion is wise, or that public opinion is unwise. Carlyle maintained that "public opinion is the greatest lie in the world," and Lincoln once said that it "generally has a strong underlying sense of justice." But a moment's thought will convince us that this common way of speaking about public opinion — as if it were an abstract political or social force — is at best unfruitful, because even when the term is used in this generalized sense, the users imply the presence of an issue or a combination of issues. Lincoln presumably meant that, over the years, the people, if allowed to express their views on issues of wide concern, will usually choose wisely and justly.

For our purposes, an issue may be defined as a contemporary situation with a likelihood of disagreement. There seems to be no useful purpose in speaking of public opinion on whether people should breathe or trees should grow; the element of controversy must be at least implied. It is also helpful to think of the issue as involving contemporary conflict, to distinguish opinion from law (as codified policy) and custom (as traditional behavior patterns).

2 *The Nature of Publics.* There must be, in the second place, a recognizable group of people concerned with the issue. This is the *public* of public opinion. The concept of a public that I adopt in this book was made famous by John Dewey, principally in *The Public and Its Problems*. Dewey said there are many publics, each consisting of individuals who together are affected by a particular action or idea. Thus, each issue creates its own public; and a particular public will normally not consist of the same individuals who make up any other public, although every individual may, at any given time, be a member of many publics. For example, a person may be a church member, a bridge player, a carpenter, a father, a rider of buses, and a member of a little theater group. When an issue concerning bridge players arises, he will join with other bridge players to form the *bridge-playing public*; and the opinion of these people becomes, for that issue, the public opinion. The following admittedly extreme example illustrates Dewey's notion that a "public" requires self-consciousness of its members, as well as a particular time and place, and an issue.

As an example [of the formation of a public], let us suppose that during a London wartime blackout fifty men were lost in the dark and fog of the night. After long wandering, one of them found that he seemed to have stumbled into a blind alley and that his

further progress was barred by walls on three sides. He then decided
to sit down and wait until the lights came on, or until the dawn appeared. Suppose that one by one, and silently, all fifty wanderers were
drawn by an inscrutable providence to the same place and that all
of them made the same decision — to await the coming of the dawn.
At this point, let us assume, fifty men were all congregated in a small
space and each was unaware of the presence of the others. A small
crowd had gathered, but we would have been unable to speak in
terms of a public, as far as any practical manifestation of behavior
was concerned. Each man would behave as if he were alone. Now
let us suppose that one of the men struck a match. Those nearest
to him then became aware of the fact that they had company, and
before long every one in the group would have recognized that fact.
From that moment, we might speak in terms of group consciousness;
and consequently, from that moment, we might expect manifesta-
tions of public opinion.[3]

We are primarily interested in the issues, and the opinions of publics
that form around the issues, that are important for the theory and practice of government. But the formation and re-formation of publics and
public opinions is by no means limited to political life; it pervades all
social behavior.

3   The Complex of Preferences in the Publics.   The third part of the
definition of public opinion, the complex of preferences, refers to the
totality of opinions on the issue by members of the public. It includes
the distribution of opinion in direction and intensity (for or against suggested courses of action related to the issue). But the expression *complex
of preferences* means more than mere direction and intensity; it means
all the imagined or measured individual opinions held by the relevant
public on all the proposals about the issue over which the public has
come into existence.

On each issue the interested public will divide into two or more
different points of view. Not all these points of view will be contradictory or mutually exclusive. The number of views that can be differentiated, however, will depend on the attitudes and previous experiences
of the individuals who make up the public, as well as the complexity of
the issue. A relatively simple issue, of interest only to a small and homogeneous public, will not generate the variety of views produced by more

complex issues. The erection in the city park of a monument to an elder statesman, if it becomes an issue at all, may produce only two points of view, but a new master plan for the city may call for a dozen or more recognizably different perspectives and judgments. In each case the total constellation of views generated on the issue is what we mean by the phrase *complex of preferences*. In an election, the complex of preferences includes the positions of all the people who are involved as participants or observers — including nonvoters and even outsiders who have opinions on the race.

The disposition of the people who "don't know" on any issue presents a difficult problem. It seems reasonable to believe that the "don't knows" consist of two kinds, (a) those who have no opinion because they do not care about the issue and (b) those who do care but have suspended judgment. Theoretically, the "don't cares" might be excluded from the complex of views at any given moment; politically, however, it is important to consider them as people who might become "do cares" and thereby change the balance in the complex of preferences. Those who care but have suspended judgment may be thought of simply as representing one view in the complex.

There are, as we know, a number of devices to reduce and make manageable the many individual opinions that public controversies give rise to. When public policy has to be made (when the issue has to be "acted on" officially), a dichotomous voting situation is structured. In elections citizens have to vote for or against a specific proposition or person. But it should be noted that that is a decision-making technique and a way of pulling together (aggregating) agreement and disagreement, not a matter of defining public opinion. Analytically, public opinion should be thought of as all points of view entertained by members of the public with regard to the pertinent issue.

4 The Expression of Opinion. The fourth important factor in our definition of public opinion is the *expression* of the various views that cluster around an issue. Words, spoken or printed, are the most common form of expression of opinion, but, at times, gestures — the clenched fist, a stiff-arm salute, even the gasp of the crowd — will suffice to express opinion.

Among the authorities, there is no agreement that public opinion must be defined in such a way that expression is required. Doob, for instance, speaks of both "internal" and "latent" public opinion. When the attitudes that people possess regarding a certain issue "are not expressed," he says, "reference can be made to *internal public opinion.*"[4]

One difficulty with Doob's concept of internal public opinion is that an internal opinion is not public. There can be no sense of identification among individuals (the sine qua non of a public) who have not made known in some way their common interest, no matter how strongly they feel these interests internally.

Doob's other variety of "unexpressed public opinion," "latent" opinion, refers to "attitudes of people regarding an issue when those attitudes have not yet been crystallized or when they are not being evoked or are not affecting behavior."[5] This is what might be called *potential* public opinion. It may be said that the term *latent public opinion* is important to describe a situation in which a considerable number of individuals hold attitudes or general predispositions that may eventually crystallize into opinions around a given issue. In one sense this is nothing more than a description of the psychological or sociopsychological matrix in which opinion is made. Yet, since political decisionmakers are interested in future as well as present states of public opinion, it is useful to recognize the idea of latent public opinion. For those who want to create or change opinions, the pattern of predispositions that are thought to exist in publics is a matter of importance. Generally, I think it appropriate in defining public opinion only to recognize that potentialities for future states of expressed opinion (that is, "latent public opinion") may be a concern of study. For public opinion at any given moment of measurement, expression is necessary.

5 Number of People Involved.   The last factor in the definition of public opinion is the *size* of the public that is interested in the issue. In our definition, the question of numbers is conveniently and deliberately hedged by the phrase *a significant number of people*, with the intention of excluding those minor issues and minor expressions of individuals that are essentially private in nature.

I want to make three points concerning the phrase *a significant number of people.* First, for the size of the public to be significant it is not necessary that a majority of the people affected by the issue hold opinions on that issue. Gallup reported in July 1969 that 58 percent of his respondents were ignorant or indecisive about the proposal to establish a system of antiballistic missiles in the United States. Undoubtedly all Americans are part of the public on the issue of a nuclear defense system, since all are affected by the costs and dangers of such a system.

Those who knew nothing about the ABM question were part of the conceptual public whether or not they knew it; however, since they had no opinion, they were not part of the public opinion on the question.

Second, the phrase *a significant number of people* does not require that a majority preference be discernible among those who do have opinions on the issue. Later I will consider in greater detail the majority-minority problem with regard to opinion-holding and the distributions of opinions among members of publics. Here it is necessary only to remind you that clear majority opinions are probably rare; until a poll or a vote is taken, the opinions on far-reaching issues are probably so numerous and varied that a majority preference does not exist; in the very act of polling or voting, however, the preferences must be structured so that a majority may be (though it doesn't have to be) evoked.

Third, effectiveness or probable effectiveness on policy is more important than mere raw numbers when considering what "a significant number of people" is. We want to know to what extent the various views held by members of the interested public are effective either in creating or in changing preferences of persons already members of the public, or in attracting nonmembers into the public. In short, does the complex of preferences on the issue have any effect, or is it capable of having an effect, upon the opinions or behavior of those who are not members of that public, or of members who do not yet have opinions? Since the political scientist is primarily interested in the effect of opinion upon political decisions, this problem is usually posed in terms of the influence of public opinion on the making of policy. Analysts who stress the effectiveness, or probable effectiveness, of opinions for public policy are likely to agree with Lowell's dictum that "individual views are always to some extent weighed as well as counted."[6]

We may say then that *a significant number of people* means, in each case, a different and perhaps unascertainable number; the presumption is simply that this number is capable of producing some effect — an effect that is as much a result of the intensity of opinion and the organization of effort as it is of the sheer size of the public.

DEMOCRACY AND THE OPINION-POLICY PROCESS

Once more: *Public opinion is the complex of preferences expressed by a significant number of people on an issue of general importance.*

This section is about the meaning and importance of public opinion for the life of the democratic polity ("polity" = political community). We are not concerned here with whether there could be a public opinion in nondemocratic polities — that is, in political communities where the people have few rights to speak, move, organize, or participate in making public policy.

Where citizens are relatively free to express unorthodox ideas, and to organize for change, we may expect some correspondence between what publics think and what governments do. Of course, autocratic governments *may be* reflective of, or responsive to, citizen opinion, but that is not a necessary part of the operation of such governments. On the other hand, attention to public opinion is an essential ingredient of democratic government. This section deals with opinions and democratic policy-making, principally that in our own democracy.

Opinions and Policy Oversimplified

The *opinion-policy process* is the way in which what people think is related to what government does; no more complicated idea is intended. The definition is deceptively simple. The obvious model for this view is the small, self-contained, homogeneous community where public opinion and democratic practice are seen in their simplest form: the New England town. At the town meeting, when more than half of the voters' hands go up, the policy is decided; and it might be said that public opinion has declared itself. But has it? At best it can only be said that a majority opinion, on that issue, at that moment in time, has been declared.

The New England town meeting, favorite example of democratic theorists in America, only serves to indicate that there is no simple relationship between public opinion and democratic practice.[7] Traditional ideas of citizen opinions in a democracy tend to ignore both custom and emotion, tend to assume faultless social communication, and tend to require omnicompetent generalists of the voters. Such ideas ask too much, and are not applicable, in anything like their ideal forms, in modern, industrialized, urbanized, and specialized societies.

Democratic theories developed in the eighteenth and nineteenth centuries were based on an extreme and unrealistic individualism. Early democratic thinkers presupposed a society in which the relations of rulers and ruled were those of person to person; of agent to principal, in the legal sense; and of equal to equal, in the sense of natural rights. In their thinking they tended to de-emphasize, if not abolish conceptually, all of the group relationships that bind society together and so strongly influence individual behavior. The political animal stood alone, being responsible to and influenced by nothing but reason, conscience, and rights. The opinions held as an individual were to be somehow (perhaps by majority vote alone) translated into policy — a policy that was supposed to serve the interests of the whole by serving the interests of the individual. All such theories largely ignored the rich and complex group relations that existed even in the agricultural society of 1800 and that today determine and condition the opinions of the individual in so many ways.

Traditional democratic theory also assumed, in addition to the "sociological nakedness" of the individual, that each member of the electorate would be interested in the issues, motivated by principle, aware of all the pertinent facts, and capable of choosing rationally. But the evidence is undeniable that voters today do not all have an interest in public issues. On the contrary, the "don't care" group on many issues runs as high as the "do care" group. Nor is the average voter motivated by principle — that is, by some guiding belief or value by which public issues can be judged; the evidence seems to be that sheer party habit is the most important influence on American voters.[8] Although more people call themselves "independents" nowadays, there is reason to believe that party tradition and habit, not reason and principle, are the primary determinants of political behavior in our democracy.

Nor do voters have any but the scantiest knowledge of public issues, or of those background facts necessary to form opinion that, in the light of the principles applied, make sense and are capable of being defended intelligently. In September 1963, when the Senate started debate on the nuclear test ban treaty, 22 percent of adult Americans were not aware of it, even though it had been the subject of daily headlines for six months and a nationwide TV address by President Kennedy.

If we define democracy in such a way as to set high performance standards for individual citizens — requiring them to be knowledgeable, motivated, reflective, and rational — then we will not find democracy in America or in any other large polity. However, we do not need to require that every person have these model democratic virtues, but only that in the collective or statistical sense they must be operative in the formulation of policy. Thus, though a political psychology, focusing on the qualities of the individual voter, does not offer us a picture of the democratic *person*, a political sociology, focusing on the qualities that exist collectively in the society, may give us a glimpse of a democratic *polity*.

To get a broad view of what such a democratic political community (polity) might be, we need to understand what is required for making policy democratically.

Sociological and Institutional Factors Prerequisite to Opinion Formation in Democracy

One testimony to the unity of democratic thought lies in the fact that all writers, traditional and modern alike, agree on the necessity for certain sociological and environmental conditions in the operation of popular government. Among these conditions, invariably, is the maintenance of some basic agreement of values and goals.

Homogeneity of Values and Interests.   The earlier writers phrased this precondition in terms of a uniform moral and ethical code and a shared conception of public interest. The traditional point of view is well described by Lippmann. In this classic work on public opinion, he says of Jefferson and others that "In the self-contained community, one could assume, or at least did assume, a homogeneous code of morals. The only place, therefore, for differences of opinion was in the logical application of accepted standards to accepted facts."[9]

It is quite probable that there was a high measure of value agreement (at least among the franchised) in 1800. Those who did not agree with the moral code could always move on to the frontier. The relatively small, simple agricultural communities of that time probably demonstrated sufficient solidarity of interests and ideals to make this a reasonable precondition for democratic practice. It is also probable that the same degree of homogeneity does not exist today in any of the industrialized societies that describe themselves as democracies.

It may not be entirely necessary for a democracy to have common moral codes or values. Modern writers tend to describe the minimal precondition in terms of procedural consensus and the relative maximization of individual values within agreed-upon institutions. Berelson has described the necessary homogeneity in these terms:

Liberal democracy is more than a political system in which individual voters and political institutions operate. For political democracy to survive, other features are required; the intensity of conflict must be limited, the rate of change must be restrained, stability in the social and economic structure must be maintained, a pluralistic social organization must exist, and a basic consensus must bind together the contending parties.[10]

The nature and extent of the basic moral and political values and procedures that must be commonly accepted are not clearly understood. James W. Prothro and Charles M. Grigg conducted a careful field study to gather evidence on the extent of consensus in two American communities. Ninety-five to 98 percent of their respondents agreed on basic democratic statements such as "Public officials should be chosen by majority vote" and "The minority should be free to criticize majority decisions." If agreement to this kind of culturally prescribed abstraction is what is meant by substantive consensus, then the American democracy seems to have it. But when more specific statements were derived from these generalizations, Prothro and Grigg found that "consensus breaks down completely," and that "respondents in both communities are closer to perfect discord than to perfect consensus on over half the statements."[11] This study leads the authors to conclude that agreement on democratic principles is unnecessary beyond the most general, superficial, and verbal levels.

Beyond some minimal agreement on values and interests, viable democracy is usually understood to rely upon the following institutional and environmental factors: (a) freedom of communication, (b) time for deliberation, and (c) continuing nonpartisan administrative procedures. These factors constitute what might today be called the elements of the democratic belief. These elements are critical to democracy. That they may be consciously understood and believed in by all the people is unnecessary; that they be understood by those who play influential roles in the opinion-policy process, and be acquiesced in by the rest, seems vital to the maintenance of a workable democracy.

Freedom of Communication. There has always been agreement among democrats, traditional and modern alike, that freedom of communication is one of the basic sociological factors upon which democratic discussion and decision-making depend. The precise limits of this freedom, and the extent to which the individual must be able to speak or write, have been debated by many over the years — and must be debated anew by each generation of democrats. But there has never been any doubt that on public matters each person must be allowed to think, and say, anything that does not deny to others a like freedom. On this principle, no further generalization is either necessary or possible. Its application in any community that aspires to democracy is a matter of specific historical and sociological conditions and cannot be pursued here.

Time for Deliberation.   That there must be sufficient time for the public in a democracy to consider all the relevant facts in the detail demanded by the occasion is another procedural principle that follows inescapably from the premise that the people shall in some way cooperate in making policy. In Jefferson's day, it might not have been open to doubt that there was time for deliberation in solving public problems; but this factor may no longer be taken for granted. The probability seems to be that modern technology has placed democracy at a serious disadvantage in its struggle for survival against antidemocratic ideas and powers. Technology is not all on one side. But, on balance, it appears that radio and television can only shorten to some limited extent the time that democracies require for careful discussion of public policy.

Continuing Nonpartisan Administrative Procedures.   It seems quite certain that neither Thomas Paine nor any of his friends in the formative period of democratic thought ever used the rather stuffy phrase "continuing nonpartisan administrative procedures." But they thought about this requirement for democratic practice, and they described it as the necessity for good faith and the willingness to carry out as well as to revise majority decision. The essence of this factor is that there must be known and accepted ways for changing policies and changing majorities. It is, of course, related to the ideas of freedom of communication and time for deliberation, but it is more than either of these. It is the notion that the government must have power to govern, although this power is limited and temporary, and that devices must exist for changing the government and the policy in nonrevolutionary ways. This factor was no less necessary (although it was simpler) in 1800 than it is today. Fortunately, in those democracies that have a relatively long history of nonviolent party rivalry and some agreement about bureaucratic impartiality, this requirement for democratic practice appears to be a matter of procedural consensus confirmed in usage. For new democracies, the possibility that this requirement may not be forthcoming is a real and constant threat.

PUBLIC OPINION AND PLURALIST DEMOCRACY

We have seen that the a priori requirements in traditional democratic theory are unrealistic norms for individual political behavior and quite at odds with observed citizen participation in the opinion-policy process. Yet we in the United States and the people in perhaps a dozen other countries have governments that are in large manner democratic — that demonstrate responsiveness to popular desires, protection of individual liberties, and the other broad imperatives demanded by democratic thought.

This apparent paradox has in recent years been widely recognized and at least partially resolved through a re-examination and revision that makes democratic theory more consistent with the facts of modern life. As a basis for thinking about the opinion-policy process in America we need to review briefly the main elements of the pluralistic society.

The Fundamental Importance of Groups

An individual may believe that, in the words of Sancho Panza, "Naked came I into this world, and naked shall I go out." But during the whole of life, one is subject to hundreds of sometimes conflicting, sometimes complementary group memberships and interrelations. The postulate of sociological nakedness laid down by the pioneer democrats is not now and never was consistent with the facts of human life. On the contrary, the basic fact with which all social analysis starts — especially analysis of those modern political societies that are our major concern here — is the mutual interaction and influence of individuals and groups.

We may categorize the groups in our society into five basic types: (a) kinship, (b) economic, (c) moralistic-ritualistic, (d) artistic-recreational, and (e) political.

Kinship groups are determined by blood or marriage ties of an immediate or extensive nature, the principal identifiable groups in primitive

societies. Even in modern societies these groups may be the most important, although they are relatively less stable and less permanent than in
simple societies. Insofar as kinship groups remain the basic transmitters
of social norms and traditions, and continue to be the chief socializer
of the child, they have first place among the groups in which individuals
share values and expectations.

Economic groups, in the sense in which we know them in modern
society, are largely a result of the specialization of labor and the complex
patterns of an exchange economy. However, *slaves, freemen, workers,*
and *warriors* are group distinctions (at least partly economic in origin)
known to the most ancient societies. Occupational and craft groups were
important in Western Europe at least as far back as the early Middle
Ages. In the modern democratic society it cannot be said that economic
factors determine political factors or even that there is an unfailing relationship between economic and political factors. But there are opinion
tendencies in each income and occupation group and these are subject
to reinforcement by the organization of political pressure groups.

Moralistic-ritualistic groups (churches, secret societies, and lodges,
for example) exist for the confirmation and encouragement of transcen-
dental ends. The need for an ultramaterialistic sense of purpose is so
strong in most individuals that moralistic-ritualistic groups appear to be
a necessary part of any society. They provide a ritual certainty as an
antidote to the insecurity of human life. Equally important in the Western world, they introduce an area of cooperation into a society that is
at least nominally competitive; here (at least in theory) idealism does
not have to be tempered with prudence, materialism is devalued, and no
stigma is attached to one's having been unsuccessful in competition.

Artistic-recreational groups fill the need for creativeness, beauty,
physical exercise, and camaraderie but are distinguished from the moralistic-ritualistic groups by being relatively less concerned (perhaps un-
concerned) with ethical, spiritual, or philosophical issues. Garden clubs,
athletic associations, and singing or drinking organizations are examples
that come to mind at once.

The last type, those groups overtly political in whole or part, includes
political parties (partisan organizations interested in obtaining government offices) and pressure groups (partisan or nonpartisan organizations
interested in promoting issues).[12] Political parties will normally not be
included in any of the first four categories, but a pressure group may
be — in fact, probably will be — a group of another type, only specifically
and perhaps periodically participating in the opinion-policy process.

Although this typology of groups in modern society may be conceptually useful here, it is not meant to be definitive. In the study of group organization and function, much more sophisticated classification has been and will be produced. The important point for this discussion is that public opinion is filtered, colored, and transformed in countless ways by individual and group subjectivization of fact and other opinion.

Public Opinion, the Group Struggle, and Public Policy

Gross measurements of public opinion are interesting and important, but they are not controlling factors in the determination of particular policy issues. All the pertinent studies indicate that generalized public opinion (in the manner of Gallup's national polls) is not a matter of the highest priority in legislative decision-making.[13] Whether administrators make more use than legislators of this kind of public opinion is still an open question; but the indications are that administrators, too, are more heavily influenced by specialized clientele, other officials, and pressure groups.

Gallup-type surveys between elections are important insofar as they help legislators and administrators recognize and delineate the gross limits and patterns of their political environment. Such reports are keys to the general tenor of public interest, apathy, support, or disaffection in such matters as the overall record of an incumbent, the suitability of candidates, or the fitness of political parties. These feelings of individuals, when measured and collected, might better be called public attitudes than opinions, for, as Berelson points out, they are principally matters of taste, habit, and a pattern of predispositions associated with family, social, and economic factors.[14]

The public opinion that counts in policymaking is a complex of views, group and individual, that should perhaps be called public opinions, or the opinions shared by members of publics. These opinions play upon decisionmakers in a variety of ways and in a medley of voices to influence the declared policy, which is "the equilibrium reached in the group struggle at any given moment."[15] The decisionmakers — principally legislators and administrators, but frequently the courts also — have a large measure of flexibility, as "countervailing powers" may be played off against one another. In the same way, the citizens, organized into pressure groups, are able to take advantage of the rivalries among competing leadership groups.

A MODEL OF THE OPINION-POLICY
PROCESS IN MODERN DEMOCRACY

In this synthesis I try to avoid at least some of the inadequacies of traditional theory. Thus, a democracy is defined as a governmental system in which a large electorate frequently decides upon the general tendencies of governmental action, mainly by choosing, from competing elites, officials to make specific policy. In the intervals between elections the people, individually and through groups, are encouraged to discuss and debate policy and to communicate their opinions freely to policy-making officials and their elite rivals.

The relation of public opinion to public policy may then be discussed in terms of the two major, but in no operational sense separable, problems of democratic practice: (a) the majority-minority problem and (b) the direct-representative problem.

The Majority-Minority Problem

The group theory of politics complicates, but does not abolish, the majoritarian problem in democratic practice. The question of whose interests are to be advanced in the group struggle leads inevitably to the concern for majorities and minorities. We need not go into the philosophical or moral reasons for the majoritarian principle in democratic theory. Rather, the practical reasons for the principle, and some of the operational difficulties, ought to be examined briefly in the model suggested here.

Emil Lederer has pointed out that in a democracy,

> When a decision has to be taken . . . as in voting for a political party or for a special measure, this vast complexity that forms opinion must be reduced to a clear-cut issue. The technique of every political or administrative body requires the reduction of complicated matters to a "yes" or "no"; majority rule is inevitable whenever unanimity is unattainable.[16]

This collapsing of all relevant viewpoints into a dichotomized question (or a series of dichotomized questions) is unnecessary during the period of discussion and general consideration within and among the interested publics. But as soon as a decision must be reached at any level, dichotomization is strongly indicated. Mathematically, it is difficult to obtain majority consent for policy when more than two relevant alternatives are presented, and this difficulty increases as the number of alternatives increases. Thus, as a practical matter, a democracy has to make up its mind by means of a series of either-or questions and answers: Shall we adopt Plan A or Plan B? Or, more typically, shall we adopt Plan A, "yes" or "no"? This, *at the point of decision,* is the necessary dichotomy out of which majorities are made.

Although public opinion, in its most total sense, is not majority opinion but the whole complex of views on an issue of public importance, there is apparently no way to escape calling the opinion that by a vote-counting process is carried into policy in a democracy *majority opinion.*[17] In the dichotomized situation necessary for making decisions, this leaves that less-than-half opinion, which is, again inescapably, *minority opinion.* Thus, the precompromised opinions that constitute (when compromised) the majority and minority opinions in Figure 1-1 are what we have called the complex of views of which gross public opinion is made. As soon as a policy decision is necessary in a democracy, those who decide the policy must produce a majority opinion. This opinion will be produced among the electorate itself in a direct democracy (Figure 1-1), and in the legislative body in a representative democracy (Figure 1-2).

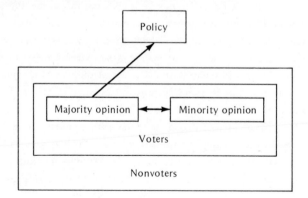

FIGURE 1-1.   Model of Opinion-Policy Process (On Issues) in Direct Democracy

The Direct-Representative Problem

Representative democracy interposes a decisionmaking body between the electorate and the public policy. But this addition of the legislative level makes the interaction of public opinion and policy considerably more complex.[18] As in the case of direct democracy, a majority and a minority opinion will be produced on each of the either-or propositions that constitute the last stage of policymaking. But in representative democracy, this simple division takes place only in the legislature. Although the complex of views that makes up general public opinion on any issue is capable of being ordered, through compromise, to produce majority and minority opinions, this is unlikely to happen; and when it does happen, the majority opinion among the public may not be the majority opinion at the legislative level. Thus we need to introduce the idea of *effective opinion*. In direct democracy, and at the legislative level in representative democracy, majority opinion is always effective opinion. But at the level of the general electorate in representative democracy, it is possible (as in Figure 1-2) for a minority coalition of individual and group opinions to become effective opinion. Examples of this case are the long-standing public support (ranging from 60 to 70 percent) for universal military training coupled with the persistent defeat of such bills in Congress, and the even longer public support for federal gun control legislation that was blocked for 28 years (1940 to 1968) by the "gun lobby" in Washington.

Effective opinion appears to turn on the degree of participation, intensity of effort, and efficiency of organization among the various individuals and groups who constitute the involved public on any particular issue. But to make this generalization is only to say that who gets what depends on who supports what points of view, how strongly they feel on the matter, and what methods are available to further their ends. Any more detailed understanding must be pursued in terms of specific issues and in the context of particular time and space. When this is done we may be able satisfactorily to identify majority, minority, and effective opinion in the given case, but our knowledge of other cases will not be furthered. Still, this generalization may offer some understanding of the overall opinion-policy process, and it may also serve as a crude matrix for the investigation of policy decisions on specific issues.

Governmental Agencies in the Opinion-Policy Process

A brief comment may help to clarify a relationship that is not explicitly shown in Figure 1-2. Lines of influence (voting and communications)

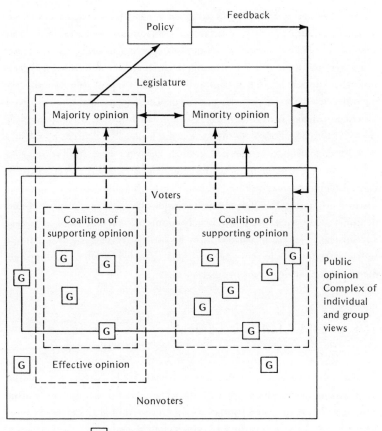

Public
opinion
Complex of
individual
and group
views

| G | Political-interest group

FIGURE 1-2.   Model of Opinion-Policy Process (On Issues) in Representative Democracy

in this schematic representation run from groups and voters to the legislature. For illustrative purposes this oversimplification seems justified. For a clearer understanding of democracy in action, however, a further point needs to be made; namely, that self-government involves a reciprocal relationship between nongovernmental networks of groups and individuals and governmental networks of groups and individuals.

This enriched view of the opinion-policy process necessitates an understanding that (a) governmental agencies other than legislatures influence (often decisively) policy outcomes, and that (b) all such governmental agencies and their individual officials may influence the continuous dialogue through which opinion and policy are shaped.

Governmental officials and agencies — especially executive and administrative but frequently judicial too — become involved as individuals and as groups in the opinion-policy process at the prelegislative level. They may be thought of as elements in the majority and minority coalitions that support legislative voting alignments. It is probable that governmental units, when participating in the group struggle, must be regulated by extraordinary restraints both self- and law-imposed; in a democracy they cannot be allowed to use the same kinds and degrees of devices permitted to nongovernmental groups. Despite these limitations, the opinion-policy process may be thought of as a two-way street. Governmental elements shape public opinion through public affairs and information programs, through the intentional effects of experimental and demonstration projects and the largely unintentional effects of countless administrative decisions in the carrying out of legislative policy, and in subtle "feedback" to nongovernmental agencies — which tailor their demands and strategies accordingly.

THE LEGISLATOR'S DILEMMA

The obligation of governmental officials to be sensitive to public opinion and, in some measure, to reflect the views of the citizens is most dramatically posed in the legislator's dilemma: Should the elected representative regard it as his duty to vote as he thinks his constituents want him to or should he exercise his independent judgment? This dilemma is one that appointed officials share, in slightly lessened degree, with elected officials; but the classic case is framed as a problem in legislative responsibility. "The bald issue," as V. O. Key, Jr., put it, "appears in the contrast between the representative bound by instructions from his constituents and the representative bound by conscience to exercise his best judgment in the interest of the nation."[19] In their interviews with legislators in four states, Wahlke, Eulau, Buchanan, and Ferguson found that legislators do in fact regard their responsibilities in one or the other of these two quite separate ways. The "delegate" role, according to this study, is adopted by legislators who tend to follow what they take to be the instructions of their constituents, and "they seem to imply that such consultation [with constituents] has a mandatory effect on their behavior." The legislator who adopts the "trustee" role "sees himself as a free agent in that, as a premise of his decision-making behavior, he claims to follow what he considers right or just, his convictions and principles, the dictates of his conscience."[20]

Although this dilemma can never be resolved as a matter of principle or "right," it may be helpful to distinguish between the representative's obligations with respect to the *values* of his constituents and his obligations with respect to the *opinions* of his constituents. Values I define here, as elsewhere in this book, as long-term, enduring, basic preferences toward objects; opinions are shorter-term and more specific orientations toward objects. It is of some use in clarifying legislators' responsibilities to say that legislators ought to try to realize the long-term value orientations of their constituents; but on matters of opinion, on which constituents are likely to change their views and on which specialized information may be available, the legislators' views ought to take primacy over those of their constituents.

The difference between voters' values and their issue positions has been empirically confirmed, in part, by Kirkpatrick's analysis of the policy views of Johnson and Goldwater supporters in 1964. Although that election was described as "issues-oriented," SRC data showed that, except for Medicare and the "values" question of whether the federal government was too strong, there was consensual overlap among all voters on all other issues. The policymaker's mandate (Johnson's in this case) could not be said to have been specific as to issues, but only general as to basic values and the direction of the opinions on issues.[21]

This difference between values and opinions seems to be, in part, what Edmund Burke had in mind when he wrote his defense of the legislator's freedom of conscience. He says of the legislator's relations with his constituents: "Their wishes ought to have great weight with him; their opinions high respect; their business unremitted attention. It is his duty to sacrifice his repose, his pleasure, his satisfaction, to theirs — and above all, ever, and in all cases, to prefer their interest to his own." Without doing too much violence to Burke's philosophy, I think one can read "their values" for "their interest" here. "But," Burke goes on, "his unbiased opinion, his mature judgment, his enlightened conscience he ought not to sacrifice to you, to any man, or to any set of men living. . . . Your representative owes you, not his industry only, but his judgment; and he betrays, instead of serving you, if he sacrifices it to your opinion."[22]

Research on the issue interests of American voters indicates a low level of understanding and concern for most questions of public policy.

In 1963 two social scientists of the University of Michigan's Survey Research Center summarized the matters as follows:

> ... most Americans are almost totally uninformed about legislative issues in Washington. At best the average citizen may be said to have some general ideas about how the country should be run, which he is able to use in responding to particular questions about what the government ought to do. For example, survey studies have shown that most people have a general (though differing) conception of how far government should go to achieve social and economic welfare objectives and that these convictions fix their response to various particular questions about actions governments might take.[23]

It seems probable, however, that in 1964 and later, American voters are becoming more knowledgeable and discriminating with regard to issues — and that they expect their representatives to take account of mass opinion distribution when policy decisions are made. One scholar believes that ". . . by and large the voting public has at least a few substantive issues in mind at the time of an election . . . . It would probably be going too far to say that the public has contextual knowledge upon which to base its decision . . . [but it] is in large measure concerned about specific issues, and these cognitions have considerable impact on electoral choice."[24] An analysis of voters' issue-interests in 1968 concludes that:

> On some issues the electorate exercises no effective constraints on leaders' policy choices. On others, the electorate permits political leaders a wide array of options at the time of the adoption of policy, while passing a retrospective judgment on such choices in subsequent elections . . . . Finally, there may be issues on which the public rather severely limits the options of leaders at the time of the adoption of policy.[25]

The author of that analysis believes that United States Vietnam policy and President Johnson's performance in office were examples of the second kind of voter limitation on policymakers; he believes race policy and "law and order" issues are examples of the third kind — on which voters very closely restrict policymakers' options.

THE OPINION-POLICY
PROCESS: GOOD OR BAD? A POSTCRIPT

Is it good or bad that in a representative democracy the opinion-policy process may make decisions contrary to majority opinion? The answer is, in the end, a matter of individual judgment. It depends how majoritarian one wants one's democracy.

Most of those who made the United States Constitution thought the potential for minority decision-making inherent in representative government was a good thing. The writers of the *Federalist Papers* defended their deliberate effort to block the effectiveness of majority opinion.[26]

But even without such deliberate efforts, representative government may frequently make minority opinion into effective opinion. As long as legislators may listen to any one of the numerous, conflicting, and inaccurately measured voices of the people, just so long may they either mistake or ignore the majority coalition of opinion. Whenever policy is made by agents (as distinguished from *plenary* policy-making in a direct democracy), the one-to-one relation of opinion and policy predicated by majoritarian democrats becomes difficult if not impossible to demonstrate.

It is doubtful, however, whether it is either theoretically or practically important that minority opinion sometimes becomes effective opinion. In the first place, majority public opinion may be wrong, in that it may adopt a position incompatible with the future operation of the democratic process. The history of civil liberties in the United States contains many minority defenses of basic democratic rights in the face of widespread, possibly majority opinions that would deny these rights.

The frequent persecutions of unpopular people and groups during national crises has been too common in American life to justify any easy assumption that public policy invariably ought to be determined by gross public opinion. The witch hunts that followed both world wars and the systematic discriminations at state and regional levels against racial, religious, and labor groups (blacks, Jehovah's Witnesses, and union organizers) have all, at certain times and places, threatened procedural and substantive rights indispensable to democracy itself. On the whole, in each of these instances of antidemocratic activity, a minority dedicated to civil liberties has defended and acted to restore democratic practice.[27]

Stouffer's study of attitudes toward civil liberties in the United States convincingly documents the greater respect for the First Amendment among the leadership minorities than among the public at large in the United States.[28] Reo Christenson summarizes the reasons why civil liberties minorities are usually successful — but why they sometimes fail:

> What democracy does need is a substantial stratum of educated persons who *do* believe in democratic processes and democratic rights and who are *willing* to work for their preservation. This stratum will necessarily be a small percentage of the total population but, because it is concerned, articulate, activist, influential with the mass media, and skilled in pressure politics, it can normally ensure that democratic values are reasonably well respected. The apathy of the average citizen ordinarily enables this stratum to wield influence far out of proportion to its numbers. But whenever the bulk of the population feels threatened from within or without, its security becomes more important to it than those rights of heretics or minorities which seem to constitute or heighten the peril. In these circumstances, no Constitution, no Supreme Court, no democratic elite can withstand a frightened or inflamed populace.[29]

There is another reason why the existence of minority-based public policy may not necessarily be bad. It is, quite simply, that policy may be changed. In the democratic society nothing is ever settled. All policies are temporary policies. And in the democratic community, as in other kinds of political communities, power makes policy. For the democrat, the issue is not the existence of the power struggle, but the political, economic, and social conditions within which the struggle takes place. These conditions and the way they are institutionalized determine whether or not the policy-making process can be termed democratic in the light of the elements described in this chapter.

Some contemporary academic and popular writers condemn American democracy because power is not so widely shared as they believe it should be. That is nothing new — perhaps, however, it is to be taken more seriously because it is old. Since the beginning of this nation some have argued for a much wider distribution of power and much greater participation by ordinary people in decisionmaking. Those eighteenth- and nineteenth-century thinkers and activists like Tom Paine and William Godwin believed, as we have seen, in a very large measure of equality. They believed in reason, the improvability (if not the perfectibility) of human beings, and in the full and direct participation of each person in political decisionmaking. Democrats like Paine and Godwin who believed in popular rule, and to whom we would now give the name "populists," would regard it as a serious flaw of the opinion-policy process if minority opinion ever became public policy. Their ideological descendants are severely critical of pluralist democracy.

The antipluralist arguments among contemporary American social theorists and activists are of two main kinds. One, based on analysis of social classes, some of which is Marxist in orientation, asserts that pluralist theories serve (intentionally or not) as apologies for domination of ordinary people by economic and political elites. Decisionmaking by compromise and trade-offs among countervailing groups is said to justify status quo interests and to make stability more important than justice and equality. Poor people and discriminated-against racial and ethnic minorities are especially disadvantaged by pluralist societies, because they do not have the resources to compete in the group struggle.

The other antipluralist argument focuses its criticism on the lack of community that pluralism implies. In pluralist democracy group interests are partial, selfish, contrived, and ungenerous. Nowhere in the pluralist version of democracy, these critics say, is there a vision of the community as a whole; nowhere is there a generous and spontaneous mode by which the individual can act out a sense of public adventure and thereby gain the highest — that is, a socially admired and acclaimed — personal fulfillment. In the works of these critics the citizen of the ideal democracy appears to be some combination of Aristotle's Athenean citizen and the modern existentialist hero.

> Politics [says Kariel] can be self-fulfilling for the knowledgeable spectator, giving him a more comprehensive perspective not because the ends attained by politics are satisfying but because politics provides a succession of progressively enriching experiences . . . . The criterion for personal action (which is simultaneously the criterion for public action) is therefore wholly pragmatic: *a decision is desirable to the extent that it facilitates comprehension of the greater diversity of experience.*[30]

It seems to me that the critics of pluralist democracy miss the mark. First, it is not true that social scientists who find pluralist democracy being practiced in America and in other industrialized polities are necessarily pleased with what they find. A descriptive statement of political conditions and processes is not an endorsement of policies produced at any given time by those conditions and processes. Many people who, using a pluralist concept of democracy as the criterion, find the United States and some other nations meeting that criterion are nevertheless dissatisfied with the achieved levels of equality, justice, and citizen participation. They too may seek to improve the conditions of life, both private and public; justice, dignity, and self-fulfillment are goals quite consistent with pluralist democracy. Further, a good case can be made, in my view, *that justice, dignity, and self-fulfillment in large and heterogeneous societies are possible only through pluralist democracy.* Versions of democracy that rest on notions of philosophical or cultural unity cannot be achieved by societies that do not have common primordial and sacred values. Only the celebration of civil values – which means the capacity to hold one's views passionately at the same time one tolerates the passionately held views of others – provides the basis for democracy in diverse societies, and that spirit can flourish only through the mutual accommodation of many groups.[31]

Thus, with regard to policy and ideology, radical pluralism is as possible as conservative pluralism. At one point in his career Chairman Mao said: "Let all flowers bloom." Whether or not he really meant it, he proclaimed the motto of radical pluralism. Indeed, why not let all flowers bloom? When each gardener, however radical or conservative, respects the flowers of all other gardeners, then diversity and participation are both maximized. Only in pluralist democracies is that happy combination possible.[32]

Notes:

[1] Jean Jacques Rousseau, "A Discourse on Political Economy," in *The Social Contract and the Discourses* (New York: E. P. Dutton & Co., 1913), p. 243.

[2] Howard Penniman, ed., *Sait's American Parties and Elections* (New York: Appleton-Century-Crofts, 1948), p. 95.

[3] Marbury Bladen Ogle, Jr., *Public Opinion and Political Dynamics* (Boston: Houghton Mifflin Company, 1950), p. 43. Reprinted by permission of Houghton Mifflin Company.

[4] Leonard W. Doob, *Public Opinion and Propaganda* (New York: Holt, Rinehart and Winston, 1948), p. 39.

[5] *Ibid.,* p. 40.

[6] A. Lawrence Lowell, *Public Opinion and Popular Government,* 2d ed. (New York: Longmans, Green and Co., 1926), pp. 13-4. See also W. Kendall and G. Carey, "The Intensity Problem and Democratic Theory," *American Political Science Review,* LXII (March 1968), 5-24.

[7] See "The conditions for town-meeting discussions" in Stanley Kelley, Jr., *Professional Public Relations and Political Power* (Baltimore, Md.: Johns Hopkins Press, 1956), pp. 225-32.

[8] In presidential elections and in the most publicized state-level elections 40 to 65 percent of Americans vote only for candidates of the party they generally favor — in less publicized local elections, partisan voting is even higher. See W. DeVries and L. Tarrance, Jr., *The Ticket-Splitter* (Grand Rapids, Mich.: W. Eerdmans Publishing Co., 1972).

[9] Walter Lippmann, *Public Opinion* (New York: Harcourt, Brace & World, Inc., 1922), p. 275.

[10] Bernard Berelson *et al., Voting* (Chicago: University of Chicago Press, 1954), p. 313.

[11] "Fundamental Principles of Democracy: Bases of Agreement and Disagreement," *Journal of Politics,* XXII (1960), 286.

[12] This follows the accepted distinction between parties and pressure groups set forth (among other places) in David Truman, *The Governmental Process* (New York: Alfred A. Knopf, Inc., 1951), pp. 33-9.

[13] See "Congressional Uses of Polls: A Symposium," *Public Opinion Quarterly,* XVIII (1954), 121-42, especially 123-29; Leonard A. Marascuilo and Harriett Amster, "Survey of 1961–1962 Congressional Polls," *Public Opinion Quarterly,* XXVIII (1964), 497-506; and Robert King and Martin Schnitzer, "Contemporary Use of Private Political Polling," *Public Opinion Quarterly,* XXXII (1968), 431-36.

[14] Berelson *et al., op. cit.,* p. 311.

[15] Earl Latham, "The Group Basis of Politics: Notes for a Theory," *American Political Science Review,* XLVI (1952), 390.

[16] "Public Opinion," in Max Ascoli and Fritz Lehmann, eds. *Political and Economic Democracy* (New York: W. W. Norton & Company, Inc., 1937), pp. 284-93, at p. 286. Lowell also stressed the need for limiting alternatives at the choosing stage. A. Lawrence Lowell, *Public Opinion in War and Peace* (Cambridge, Mass.: Harvard University Press, 1923), pp. 127-8, 134-7, 148-50.

[17] Precision requires us to distinguish legislative decisionmaking from election. The choice of one candidate, when three or more are running, is frequently an expression of what might be called *plurality opinion.*

[18] For a perceptive discussion of the difference between voting opinions and issue opinions in representative government, see Gerhart D. Wiebe, "Public Opinion between Elections," *Public Opinion Quarterly,* XXI (1957), 229-36.

[19] V. O. Key, Jr., *Public Opinion and American Democracy* (New York: Alfred A. Knopf, Inc., 1961), p. 481.

[20] John C. Wahlke, Heinz Eulau, William Buchanan, and LeRoy C. Ferguson, *The Legislative System: Explorations in Legislative Behavior* (New York: John Wiley & Sons, Inc., 1962), pp. 272, 276.

[21] Samuel A. Kirkpatrick, "Issue Orientation and Voter Choice in 1964," *The Social Science Quarterly,* XLVIII (1968), 87-102.

[22] *Burke's Politics: Selected Writings and Speeches of Edmund Burke on Reform, Revolution, and War,* ed. Ross J. S. Hoffman and Paul Levack (New York: Alfred A. Knopf, Inc., 1949), p. 115.

[23] Warren E. Miller and Donald E. Stokes, "Constituency Influence in Congress," *American Political Science Review,* LVII (1963), 47. See also Herbert McClosky *et al.,* "Issue Conflict and Consensus Among Party Leaders and Followers," *American Political Science Review,* LIV (1960), 406-27.

[24] David E. RePass, "Issue Salience and Party Choice," *American Political Science Review,* LXV (1971), 400.

[25] Richard W. Boyd, "Popular Control of Public Policy: A Normal Vote Analysis of the 1968 Election," *American Political Science Review,* LXVI (1972), 446.

[26] For instance, they declared that equal representation in the Senate would discourage "the propensity of all single and numerous assemblies to yield to the impulse of sudden and violent passions, and to be seduced by fractious leaders into intemperate and pernicious resolutions." *The Federalist, No. 62.*

[27] That minority elites may at times acquiesce in antidemocratic activity is also apparent — the ejection of duly elected socialists from the New York State Legislature in 1921 and the forced relocation of the West Coast Japanese in 1942 are cases in point. But, generally, they have been much more zealous than nonelites in maintaining the democratic environment.

[28] Samuel Stouffer, *Communism, Conformity, and Civil Liberties* (Garden City, N.Y.: Doubleday & Co., Inc., 1955), Chapter 2, "Are Civic Leaders More Tolerant Than Other People?" pp. 26-7. See also Allen H. Barton, "Consensus and Conflict Among American Leaders," *Public Opinion Quarterly,* XXXVIII (Winter 1974-1975), 507-30.

[29] Reo M. Christenson, *Heresies Right and Left: Some Political Assumptions Reexamined* (New York: Harper & Row, Publishers, 1973), pp. 41-2.

[30] Henry Kariel, *The Promise of Politics* (Englewood Cliffs, N.J.: Prentice-Hall, 1966), pp. 30-1. Italics in original.

[31] For a good discussion of primordial, sacred, and civic values, see Charles Andrain, *Political Life and Social Change,* 2d ed. (North Scituate, Mass.: Duxbury Press, 1974).

[32] "Democracy is the system of the future because democracy alone is consistent with the pluralistic and multigroup society which industrialism inevitably creates. All other types of government are essentially oligarchic, and oligarchies represent too few groups to satisfy modern pluralistic societies." — William G. Carleton, "Is Democracy to Blame?" *Virginia Quarterly Review,* XXXII (1957), 228.

2 How to Know Opinions

The measurement of public opinion is, in its simplest sense, finding out what people think. So defined, it is as old as society. As human organization evolved, social differentiation was always accompanied by some kind of communication, by gestures and verbalization, and created situations in which it was frequently important for some people to know what certain numbers of the others thought about matters of common interest. One cannot imagine a simple community without also imagining a collection of the more influential men sitting around a fire or flat rock — "council rocks" are still common landmarks wherever there were tribes of American Indians — discussing things that were important to them all.

Although the societies and the meetings were vastly different, the council of Mesopotamian warriors in 5,000 B.C. and the yearly New England town meeting served the same purposes for running society. Functionally, these meetings were similar. Each constituted, among other things, a measurement of opinion. By the time of the development of New England democracy in the seventeenth and eighteenth centuries, there were other ways of measuring opinion; there were church meetings, plenty of them; there were handbills and simple newspapers; there were officials whose job it was to communicate regularly with the people with regard to public matters. But the *meeting* and the *vote*, or the "sense of the meeting," have been fundamental ingredients in the measuring of opinion for thousands of years.

THE POLITICAL IMPORTANCE
OF OPINION MEASUREMENT

Among the power holders of every society there has been attention to the thinking and desires of the masses. Even in the time when absolutism was a fairly respectable indoor theory, no king could afford completely to ignore the wishes of the population.

It may be helpful to differentiate between what might be called positive public opinion, on the one hand, and mere acquiescence, on the other. It can be argued that all rulers of all time have needed the acquiescence of the masses, but not necessarily the support of positive public opinion. To the extent that the masses were uninterested, unable, or unwilling to think or act with regard to public affairs, positive public opinion, as we know it, was of no consequence. Until fairly recently, as anthropological history goes, the masses had no education, no information from outside their own little villages, and no human energy left over after obtaining scant physical needs. They had few or no opinions regarding public matters.

Machiavelli, whom political scientists both claim and deny as patron saint, stands more or less at the bridge between old and new. He recognized that it is useful and preferable to gain the positive support of the people but that the passive toleration of the masses is a most necessary minimum for stability. The ruler, he says, "who has but a few enemies can easily make sure of them without great scandal, but he who has the masses hostile to him can never make sure of them, and the more cruelty he employs the feebler will his authority become; so that his best remedy is to try and secure the good will of the people."[1]

POLITICAL REPRESENTATION
AND OPINION MEASUREMENT

When the number of persons whose opinions count is very small, as in primitive societies and in tiny self-governing communities, whether public or private, the opinions of all can be measured. Nonpublic organizations, such as church congregations, social clubs, and economic groups, may also conduct their business by meetings of the whole membership, by mail ballots, or by questionnaires sent to each person. As we shall see, these private primary groups constitute an important element in the larger network of public opinion. But restricting our consideration here to governmental units, we may say that only the unlimited town meeting (and perhaps some special districts of very small power and geography) can be based on the idea that the opinions of all the voters will be measured.

Size, as we know, is the limiting factor to the direct measurement of opinion. Assemblies of constituents — like town meetings or rallies — are simply not effective when there are more than three or four hundred in attendance. The member of Congress or congressional candidate cannot obtain the opinions of all voters in the district. The maker of some new detergent called Slosh cannot measure the reactions of all housewives to the product. In these cases, some kind of representation device must be introduced. The opinions of some of the people are measured, and, from those measured opinions, deductions are made about the opinions of all.

This two-step process, oversimplified here, is a form of *sampling*. Whether it is good sampling or bad sampling depends, most importantly, on whether accurate deductions can be made from the measurement of the representative group. Thus, it may be said, in a sense, that there is bad representation and good representation.

The measurement of public opinion is as important in a society as is the extent to which the support of the masses is necessary, or is thought to be necessary, for the legitimating or the operation of government. Briefly, the importance of public opinion (and, therefore, of the measurement of public opinion) depends on the degree of democracy in the society. Insofar as there are theories that say that the people have a right to influence their governments, so far is public opinion important.

As a practical matter, political leaders are selective in their assessments of public opinion. They try, first, to measure the opinions of those people who have the greatest influence on their own future and the future of those policies they must support or oppose. The legislator looks first to the opinions of the most influential people of the district.

Which persons and groups are important to officials depends not alone on the officeholders' individual beliefs and preferences but also on those notions of political representation that find acceptance in the political theory of the time. The public opinion that is measured is, politically, the opinion that is influential; and the importance of popular influence is apt to be assessed differently at different times and in different places. Although George Gallup may sometimes measure opinion that is merely interesting or curious, the politician in every time and place attempts to measure the opinion that makes a difference to the theory and practice of government.

THE SIMPLE INGREDIENTS
OF EVERYDAY OPINION MEASUREMENT

Whether opinion sampling is good or bad, it always involves *asking*, *listening*, and *reading*. Politicians ask each other, "What do you hear?" The candidate, the market researcher, the commercial pollster, and just about every active person listens constantly and interprets what is heard consciously or unconsciously, into a measurement of opinion.

The opinion measurer, whether pollster, politician, or plain citizen, can pick up many clues to the opinions of others just by listening. Asking is not necessarily associated with listening, and American social scientists have shown increasing interest in what the authors of one book call "unobtrusive measures" of attitudes and opinions.[2] But, despite the usefulness of indirect measurements, asking and listening are usually interrelated parts of efforts to understand public opinion. The politician asks friends and acquaintances and, on the basis of their responses, attempts to create a picture of public opinion. The pollster asks respondents broad or narrow questions in as much detail as is necessary.

Much measurement of opinion is done by reading. The candidate reads the district newspapers. The editor of one paper reads other papers. The entrepreneur looking for a new location for a store reads the business news, specialized suburban papers, and the public records of new subdivisions and home construction. All are, in some degree or other, sampling public opinion by reading.

This endless measuring of opinion is a process in which we all share in various degrees, for opinion-measuring is inevitable in every social situation. Most of this "horseback" opinion-measuring is of little general consequence. It is of no political importance whether a person accurately measures the opinions of others in situations that involve only private relationships. But we do care whether the official decisionmakers get a good picture of citizens' opinions on public policy.

"EAR TO THE GROUND": POLITICIANS MEASURE OPINION

We have said that all opinion measurement involves some combination of reading, asking, listening, and thinking. The person who is interested in public questions, whether government official, party activist, pressure group leader, or League of Women Voters independent, will use all these methods of assessing the views of publics. From the viewpoint of the holders of political power, keeping one's "ear to the ground" meant, before the advent of scientific polls, collecting printed and spoken opinions and discounting them according to the supposed reliability of those who enunciated them.

The politician avidly reads newspaper stories and other expressions of opinion. She reads specialized publications, such as the newsletters of organizations that operate in her area or are interested in matters that interest her. She reads mail carefully and always answers it, with greater or lesser attention, depending on who the letter is from and how it is written. Beyond this, she sees people and talks with people. She asks and listens. In short, in her measurement of opinion, she conducts informal interviews.

It seems to be true that politicians talk mainly to other politicians. They probably spend half or more of their talking time, except when they are on a planned sidewalk hunt for opinions (or more likely for votes), in conversation with other politicians. But this leaves considerable talking time for nonpoliticians — for family, for friends whose friendship is based on nonpolitical considerations, and for casual contacts. Although families and nonpolitical friends tend to get little time from politicians — the *virus politicus* is a consuming malady that allows little private life — politicians often talk to casual contacts and constituents. The American cabdriver is legendary as informant for politicians — and probably with good reason, since cabdrivers overhear and participate in many conversations with mobile and influential "opinion leaders" in our society.

Door-to-door canvassing, as a way of measuring opinions, is not new in politics. The good precinct captain has done it for years. He has not done it scientifically, using the mathematical laws of probability, but his practical judgment and knowledge of his area may be so keen that his assessments are accurate enough for his purposes. There are many stories of ward and precinct politicians who can predict the vote in their areas within one or two percentage points. This is not surprising in areas that are small, and intensively "worked."

An early attempt to assess the ability of party politicians to predict elections was made by Claude E. Robinson in 1932. He collected two types of data from the presidential election campaign of 1928. First, he gathered Republican estimates by county from three states. He compared these forecasts with the actual elections returns, and calculated the "plurality error" (the difference between the *estimated* plurality and the *actual* plurality) for each county. He found that the plurality errors ranged from 0.1 percent to 52 percent, and that the average plurality error by county was 13 percent for two of the states and 14 percent for the other.[3] Second, from a number of political leaders and newspapermen, Robinson compiled a list of estimates by state and political party. He listed "trustworthy" estimates of Democrats in eight states, and found that their median plurality error in 1928 was 18 percent; Republican estimates in sixteen states showed much better predictive validity, having a median plurality error of only 7 percent.[4]

The differences between their predictions and the actual vote is striking testimony to the proposition that politicians tell themselves what they want to hear. Robinson says that politicians, in estimating their future, suffer from the "elation complex." He says that this is a necessary self-delusion, for "men who believe they are whipped are almost sure to be beaten"; but it "constitutes the chief weakness in the predictive technique of the politician," for it "opens the door to delusions of grandeur and power, and causes otherwise normal men to see great and sweeping victories where fate holds crushing defeat in store."[5]

STRAW POLLS

Claude E. Robinson says that a straw poll is "an unofficial canvass of an electorate to determine the division of popular sentiment on public issues or on candidates for public office."[6] The first known attempts to measure electoral opinion on a mass scale were the so-called "straw polls" developed by newspapers in the nineteenth century.

In the summer of 1824 the *Harrisburg Pennsylvanian* sent out reporters to check on popular support for the four presidential contenders of that year. On July 24 the paper reported that a "straw vote taken without discrimination of parties" showed Jackson to be the popular choice over John Quincy Adams, Henry Clay, and William H. Crawford.[7]

Polling and political prediction has been, as the *Encyclopaedia Britannica* declares, "an intermittent practice of U.S. journalism"[8] during the past 150 years. Toward the end of the nineteenth century the *New York Herald* became more regular in its forecasts for local and state as well as national elections. During presidential campaigns the *Herald* collected estimates from newsmen and political leaders in many parts of the country and predicted the electoral college votes by state. In 1908 that paper began a collaborative effort with Cincinnati, Chicago, and St. Louis papers. Later their group was joined by three other papers (in Boston, Denver, and Los Angeles), conducting polls in thirty-seven states in 1912 and thirty-six in 1916. Other papers and some magazines, including the *Farm Journal*, began in the same period to make election predictions based upon opinion surveys of one kind or another. By 1920 it was clear that straw polling was more than an "intermittent practice."

The chief problem in straw polling, as commonly conducted, is that it is almost impossible to ensure that the persons giving their opinions are representative of all the people whose opinions are presumably being measured. There is no certainty that the microcosm (the sample) is like the macrocosm (the universe). For instance, straw polls are often conducted through the distribution of ballots in commercial or recreational places; the ballots are marked by those who care to mark them, and the results are tabulated by the conductor of the poll.

The best-known straw poll of this century was that conducted by the *Literary Digest* magazine from 1916 to 1936. In the Hughes-Wilson presidential contest in 1916, the *Digest* asked its readers simply to send information about popular sentiment; it also took a poll among its subscribers in the five key states of Illinois, Indiana, New Jersey, New York, and Ohio. In 1920 the *Digest* mailed 11,000,000 ballot cards to test public reaction to possible presidential candidates; this was, in a sense, an unofficial presidential primary. In the fall of 1924 the magazine mailed 16,500,000 ballots to owners of telephones and automobiles in the United States, asking their choice between the presidential candidates of that year. In the presidential poll of 1928 more than 18,000,000 ballots were mailed. Furthermore, the *Literary Digest* conducted three nationwide polls on prohibition, in 1922, 1930, and 1932.

Although the *Digest* polls were widely quoted and commented upon by other magazines and newspapers, the chief reason for their establishment and growth seems to have been their advertising and subscription-getting value. With each ballot card a subscription blank was mailed to the prospective straw voter. Robinson reports that "as a result of the 1930 postcard poll on prohibition, which was mailed to 20,000,000 people throughout the nation, the *Literary Digest* . . . was able to say, 'Almost overnight we have advanced circulation tremendously.'"[9]

The *Literary Digest* flourished during the 1920s and early 1930s. The elections of 1924, 1928, and 1932 were accurately predicted, and there seems to be some evidence (when measured against official referendums in ten states) that the polls on the prohibition amendment caught the trend in favor of repeal between 1926 and 1932.

But in 1936, after its gigantic blunder of predicting an electoral college majority for the Republican presidential nominee, Alfred M. Landon, the *Literary Digest* went out of the polling business forever. Shortly thereafter, in 1938, it went out of *all* business forever.

What has happened since 1936 — and it is a most significant development for opinion measurement, as we shall see next — has been the combination of field interviewing of people with probability mathematics in the creation of a whole new science of survey research.

The political application of survey research and especially the use of polls by officeholders and candidates are now thoroughly accepted in American life. But it should not be thought that informal, everyday, and intuitive measurement of opinions has disappeared from politics. The world of candidates and managers is one in which they have to make multiple measurements, attentive to signs and clues of all kinds, judging as they go what actions are likely to be productive or unproductive for them. Into such a world scientific polling has now in the 1970s, been thoroughly accepted. But the details, the doubts, the confidences, and all the existential "feel" of politicians for their political milieu still inform the creation, the interpretation, and the use of scientific polling.

SURVEY RESEARCH

The objective of public opinion surveys is to obtain responses to uniform questions from a select number of persons (the sample) who, according to criteria thought to be relevant, are representative of the whole group of people (the universe) about whom one wants information. The sample, then, ought to be an exact miniature of the universe or it ought to be constructed so that the ways in which it differs from the universe will lead to valid information about the universe.

In the first instance, suppose that the pollster wants to study class feeling about price controls in a country in which 30 percent of the population are in the lower socioeconomic class, 55 percent are in the middle, and 15 percent are in the upper. If the pollster is limited to two thousand interviews, it will be necessary to seek out six hundred persons in the lower class, eleven hundred in the middle, and three hundred in the upper class. Assuming that other measures are taken to prevent bias, a sample will be obtained that, on class lines, is as nearly like the universe as can be. The results can then be projected directly to the whole universe with some expectation of accuracy.

Suppose, however, that the purpose of the study is to learn about the popular acceptance or rejection of government price controls. The pollster may then reason that the views of the upper class are more significant for policymaking — first, because of the direct impact of these views on governmental decisions, and, second, because of their influence on the views of the middle and lower classes — and it may be decided, therefore, to oversample the upper-class segment. In this way one deliberately constructs a sample that is not representative of the socioeconomic universe, in order to obtain a sample that is more representative of the universe of influence — which in this case is more important than mere socioeconomic correspondence between the sample and the universe.[10]

In the construction of a scientific public opinion survey, several distinct steps may be seen:

1. Statement of information desired.
2. Identification of the universe.
3. Determination of sample size and type.
4. Construction of the questionnaire.
5. Recruitment and training of interviewers.
6. Fieldwork.
7. Processing and analysis of data.

These steps are not all of equal magnitude, nor are they equally demanding of the time and energy of the pollster. However, it can be argued that they are of equal importance, since, like the links of a chain, each is vital to all. No matter how precise and sophisticated the theoretical formulation of sample and questionnaire, if there is any breakdown in the steps involving the collection, processing, or analysis of data, the survey fails. In turn, if the right questions are not asked of the right people, perfection in other steps is fruitless.

Statement of Information Desired

All too frequently, students begin fieldwork in public opinion without any but the foggiest notion of what they want to find out. Given the somewhat artificial situation in which such "laboratory practice" occurs, this is perhaps not too surprising. But it is surprising to find, as one often does in political polling — and as is said to be the case in commercial market research — that persons who have a real need for survey work are sometimes unable, at first, to say what they want to discover.

If the candidate is to spend money wisely, the pollster must be told what kinds of information are wanted from what kinds of people in the constituency. For instance, if one wants to know what issues and themes to stress in a campaign, it is of little worth to gather responses about the public image of one's opponent — the question "What is there about Mr. X that you especially like or don't like?" will not evoke responses that can be used as guidelines for a whole campaign. The responses may give valuable hints on how to exploit an opponent's weaknesses, but they will tell nothing about what issues may interest the electorate.

Suppose the mayor or the city manager asks the pollster to find out whether the residents are in favor of slum clearance and urban renewal, and the pollster reports a good response to such questions as "Would you favor the redevelopment of the Old Town section?" Nevertheless, the mayor's proposal may be defeated in the referendum to authorize the project because the pollster did not ask the citizens "Would you support a $200,000,000 bond for the redevelopment project?" and because the residents of the Old Town area were not asked whether they would be willing to live elsewhere if necessary. This kind of error can hardly be blamed on the pollster — although, in these exaggerated examples, it is apparent that some of the fault would lie there for failing to help the client define the goals.[11]

Identification of the Universe

Whose opinions are to be sampled?

To gather information about possible ways of increasing its circulation by changing contents, should a magazine sample its readers or its nonreaders? To learn the tastes in styling of potential buyers of its Cadillacs, should General Motors choose a sample from below the $10,000-income class or from above $20,000-income class? Should it interview only men in the selected income group, as many women as men, or 70 percent women? Should the candidate take as her universe the potential voters in her constituency or only the habitual voters or (for primary elections) only those who are registered in her party?

The question of whose opinions to measure, like the question of what information is desired, depends on the factors of the individual case. Public opinion surveys are not, and never will be, substitutes for thinking about social cause and effect, or for decisions based on facts and opinions that are not derived from opinion surveys. The opinion survey is a tool, with clear limits of usefulness and no magic whatever.

Sample Size

The number of people to be interviewed in any poll depends in part on the importance that the sponsors place on being able to make an accurate prediction and on the money available for the conduct of the poll.

Public opinion surveys are expensive. You will discover why if you undertake fieldwork; even the best interviewer cannot gather many interviews in a day, if he uses the techniques that keep distortion at a minimum.

Ignoring for the moment that cost is an important limiting factor, how large should the sample be? The answer is that *the sample should be large enough to ensure that the results are within those limits of chance error that satisfy the sponsor.*

To explain this answer, we must refer to the mathematics of probability. If we assume (a) that there is a real but unknown distribution of all possible answers to a question, (b) that our sample is random (every person is just as likely to be chosen as every other person), and (c) that our techniques are capable of obtaining the true opinion from each person — if we assume all these things, we will be able to tell how accurate the responses are.

The size of the sample is not the major source of error in most opinion surveys. When errors occur, in almost every case it is not because too few persons were interviewed, but because the wrong persons were wrongly interviewed. The effective use of relatively small samples is illustrated in the polling before the 1960 and 1972 presidential elections. The major nationwide poll forecasts were all within two percentage points of the actual vote (see Table 2-1).

A sample of a few thousand — or maybe even one thousand — is capable, statistically, of producing an accurate reflection of the opinions of a hundred million or more people. Contrary to what may appear to be common sense, very large samples (say ten thousand to fifty thousand) are not much more accurate than medium-sized samples (fifteen hundred to five thousand), and the improved results of such large samples are almost never worth their costs.

For the purposes of any class projects in which you might be engaged, carefully constructed samples of one hundred to five hundred cases will usually result in a low enough chance error. When your project involves a fairly small universe (a ward, a legislative district, a small city, a county, or even several counties), the size of your sample need not be very large to obtain reasonably reliable results — provided, always, that you have selected the persons to be interviewed according to relevant criteria.[12] The best handbooks for undergraduate research design are Earl R. Babbie, *Survey Research Methods* (Wadsworth Publishing Co., 1973) and Charles H. Backstrom and Gerald D. Hursh, *Survey Research* (Northwestern University Press, 1963).

Sample Selection

More important than the size of the sample, beyond some minimum, is the type of sample chosen. Early straw pollsters interviewed anyone they happened to meet. The so-called inquiring reporters still talk to people they haphazardly encounter. But serious attempts to measure opinion always involve interviewing people who are in some sense representative. Representativeness in a sample is ensured only by randomness alone or by some combination of stratification and randomness. Randomness means that each unit of the universe has an equal chance of being drawn into the sample. Stratification is the division of the universe according to criteria the pollster thinks relevant.

TABLE 2-1.　Percentage Error of Forecasts by Major Polls in 1960, 1964, 1968, and 1972 Presidential Elections

1960 Polls	Sample Size	Predictions		Results		Percentage Error
		Kennedy	Nixon	Kennedy	Nixon	
Gallup	8,000	51.0	49.0	50.1	49.9	0.90
Roper	3,000	48.94	51.06	50.1	49.9	1.16
John Kraft	2,000	51.58	48.42	50.1	49.9	1.48
Princeton Research Service	Not available	52.0	48.0	50.1	49.9	1.90

1964 Polls	Sample Size	Predictions		Results		Percentage Error
		Johnson	Goldwater	Johnson	Goldwater	
Gallup	Not available	64.0	36.0	61.4	38.6	2.60
Harris	Not available	64.0	36.0	61.4	38.6	2.60

1968 Polls	Sample Size	Predictions			Results			Percentage Error*
		Nixon	Humphrey	Wallace	Nixon	Humphrey	Wallace	
Gallup	2,800	43.0	42.0	15.0	43.4	42.9	13.6	0.40
Harris (11/4/68)†	2,559	43.0	39.8	17.2	43.4	42.9	13.6	0.40
Harris (11/5/68)†	1,206	40.0	43.0	13.0	43.4	42.9	13.6	3.40

1972 Polls	Sample Size	Predictions		Results		Percentage Error
		Nixon	McGovern	Nixon	McGovern	
Gallup (11/6/72)	3,500	62.0	38.0	61.8	38.2	0.20
Harris (11/6/72)	Not available	60.0	37.0	61.8	38.2	1.80
Yankelovich (10/30/72)# (New York Times Pollster)	"Approx. 1,500"	65.0	36.0	61.8	38.2	3.20

*Because of George Wallace's third-party candidacy, the 1968 predictions and poll errors are less clear. Nixon got 43.4 percent of the national popular vote, and the errors are calculated on that figure.

†Harris' release on November 4 included interviews through the Friday (November 1) before election day. His release on November 5 (election day) included interviews through the Sunday (November 3) before election. He claimed his Monday (Nov. 4) release reflected a last-minute swing sufficient to elect Humphrey; Nixon's campaign manager charged that Harris was attempting to influence the election on Humphrey's behalf.

#The Yankelovich polls are not strictly comparable. They consisted of telephone interviews with potential voters in 16 states important in the electoral college.

A hypothetical case may help to explain how randomness and stratification are used. A United States senatorial candidate from New Jersey
has, let us say, a universe that consists of all registered voters in the state.
He could have the name of each voter put in a capsule to be whirled in
a cage, then he could blindly pick out 1,000 names to be interviewed. He
then would have a pure random sample.

But let us suppose our New Jersey senatorial candidate also knows
(as is the case) that the youngest and oldest voters are less likely to vote
than those in the middle-age groups, that women are less likely to vote
than men, and that those with incomes under $7,500 are less likely to
vote than those with incomes over $7,500. If the candidate is able to
obtain the relevant data from the voter registration lists or census, he
may want to divide his total universe into subgroups, or strata, drawing
into his sample proportionately more middle-aged registrants, more men,
and more from the over-$7,500 stratum. If he does so, he might be able
to obtain the same accuracy with 900 persons in this stratified sample
that he would get in the 1,000-person pure random sample first mentioned.[13] The decision to stratify in some ways rather than other ways
is always a human judgment, based on the relatedness of the stratification
factors to the information desired.

The candidate, assessing his strength and the issues in his constituency, may want to know how he is faring among men and women voters
and among voters in different age groups, economic brackets, and ethnic
or religious groups, and maybe those in different education or professional groups. If he is running for mayor of a mining town where there
are sixty men for every forty women, it will not do for him to sample
homes on weekday afternoons or to be satisfied with a stratification
that results in a sample consisting of 60 percent of women.

In general, pollsters consider their research design and what they
want to find out, then say to themselves something like this: "For the
ideas we are trying to test or the kinds of information we hope to get,
what kinds of people do we want to interview?" This, in a homely, overall way, is what we mean by selecting relevant attributes for stratifying
the sample.

"Quota Control" Samples. From 1936 to 1948 the national polling
organizations almost exclusively used a system of sample selection called
quota control. In that system interviewers are expected to choose in
their areas a certain number of persons who fall within predetermined

categories, such as class, sex, race, partisanship, place of residence, and so forth. (The categories overlap, of course, and one interview may produce a low-income Democratic farmer.) Quota sampling has inherent and obvious potentiality for error. Interviewers cannot be expected to choose the "right" respondents, even when given explicit instructions about the numbers of persons to be interviewed from each categorical group. The interviewer may consciously or unconsciously bias the selections.

The experience of all polling organizations is that interviewers who are allowed to choose their respondents tend to undersample the poor, the less well educated, and the racial and ethnic minorities. To minimize this bias, some of the polling organizations attempt to reduce the interviewer's discretion in choosing respondents within the quota. They may require a certain percentage of evening interviews (especially from their women interviewers), or they may require that all interviewing be done in the respondent's home or that no more than two interviews be obtained in any one block.

"Area Random" Samples. Despite such efforts to reduce bias in the selection of respondents, quota sampling is generally held to be more error-prone than sampling systems that designate all the individuals to be interviewed. Such systems are sometimes called *pinpoint* or *specific-assignment* sampling, but the most common and useful term seems to be *area random.* Whatever term is used, it should be remembered for this discussion that the important feature, the one that distinguishes this method from quota control, is that all individual respondents are predetermined by the survey designers either through purposive and systematic selection or by a series of random choices.

The first step in creating an area sample is the division of the universe into smaller units, called *primary sampling areas.* The selections of these primary sampling areas may be the result of judgments relating to the hypotheses or information to be studied. Of the six hundred precincts in a city, twenty may be chosen for political, economic, ethnic, or other reasons related to the study. Or the primary sampling units may be chosen by chance methods — for example, by taking every thirtieth precinct (*selection by constant intervals*) or by drawing the thirty numbers out of a hat (*random selection*). If chance methods are used, all parts of the universe must be covered by the smaller areas (with no overlap), and each of the smaller areas must have as good a chance of being selected as any other.

For samples drawn from a large geographical universe, such as the whole United States, it is often desirable to choose secondary or sub-sampling areas. Thus, the primary sampling areas might be six hundred of the more than three thousand counties in the nation. From these six hundred units, thirty secondary sampling areas (cities, parts of cities, and townships) might be drawn. When intermediate areas of this kind are used, they should be selected, like the primary areas, purposively or by chance.

The next step in obtaining an area random sample is the determination of all the dwelling units within the chosen geographical areas from which the individual respondents are to be selected. Sometimes these can be determined from public or quasi-public sources — from city or county maps, directories or lists, or from the records of utilities or construction companies. Often, however, it may be necessary for the field staff (perhaps the interviewers themselves) to locate every dwelling unit in the sampling areas.

Next, a number of dwelling units are chosen, almost always by constant-interval or random selection, from the complete list of such units. Finally, a particular person is designated in each of the chosen dwelling units. All such persons together constitute the sample.

Construction of the Questionnaire

In this section, please think of the questionnaire as meaning, in general, the total of all the questions asked — or, even more broadly, as the total material used for the elicitation of responses from each person interviewed. Normally, the questionnaire will consist of one or more printed, mimeographed, or typewritten sheets on which questions are written. But, in some surveys, cards, posters, or other display materials may be used to clarify or enlarge upon the written or spoken questions or to increase interviewing uniformity and reliability. When such supplementary items are used they should be thought of as part of the questionnaire.

Questionnaires are so much a part of our everyday life that it may seem, at first, that the construction of such a list of questions is a task that any reasonably well-educated and honest person could do as effectively as any other. One is tempted to believe that straightforward answers can be evoked by simple, straightforward questions. Unfortunately, this is not always so. Aside from the vagaries of English (and all other languages), each questionnaire constructor and each respondent brings to each question particular and often highly unusual meanings and nuances. One does not have to be a semanticist to appreciate, after the shortest attempt at question construction, the significance of what Stuart Chase calls "the tyranny of words."

Structurally, there are three kinds of questions asked in public opinion studies: *dichotomous, multiple-choice,* and *open-end.*

The dichotomous question is, like the pawn, both lowly in rank and vital to the game. Dichotomous means, simply, two-sided: *yes-no, true-false, plus-minus.* Though the limitations of the dichotomous question are clear, it has great importance for all kinds of simple fact- and opinion-gathering. It is used especially in obtaining biographical or census-type data: "Are you married? Do you own your home? Are you a registered voter? Do you belong to a labor union?"

The multiple-choice question is a type with many subtypes, such as checklists, rank orderings, and matching-answer questions. Sometimes referred to as the "cafeteria" question, it gives the respondent some alternatives beyond the very confining yes-no choice of the dichotomous question. On the other side, however, it avoids the utter subjectivity and nearly insoluble problems of coding and analysis that open-end questions give rise to. It is widely used in public opinion research precisely because it is a compromise, structurally, between the other two types.

Open-end questions are answered in the respondent's words and style. Because the answers are wholly idiosyncratic, they cannot be analyzed with complete precision. However, what is lost in analytical precision is gained in richness and subtlety of response. In the hands of skilled interpreters, enough responses can be categorized to make for analyses that are frequently more penetrating, and possibly more valid, than the rigid results of dichotomous or multiple-choice questions. Nevertheless, generalizations are hazardous, and outside advice may be a disservice to the investigator who wants to know when to employ open-end questions; his own thoughtful judgment is the best guide.

A good questionnaire uses words, insofar as possible, in the way the respondents use them. Thus, technical and rarely used words are to be avoided. The form of the questionnaire should be conversational. Don't ask: "For whom do you intend to vote?" Most people don't talk that way. Ask: "Who do you intend to vote for?" or "Who do you think you'll vote for?"

Finally, good survey research avoids questions that are "loaded" or "leading" — that is, questions that tend to predetermine the answers. Questions are often loaded by the inclusion of references to widely accepted cultural values.[14] I was once part of a survey research team that asked Wisconsin farmers whether they regarded their children's chores "more as a duty or for teaching them responsibility." That was bad phrasing. Only one or two out of every one hundred farmers replied that chores were a duty. The idea of teaching children responsibility in a democracy had been driven home to these respondents through all the channels by which attitudes are shaped in our society; those who might have thought that it was a duty for children to work for parents could hardly have been expected to say so. People tend to give the respectable answer, or the answer they think the interviewer wants to hear, when their own self-respect is involved or when the questions are on matters about which they have no knowledge of feelings. Thus, unwed mothers are apt to exaggerate their attachment to conventional norms about premarital sex,[15] and poorly educated or poorly informed respondents often give inconsistent and ambiguous answers to questions about political or social matters on which they think they should have opinions but in fact do not.[16]

Sometimes indirection is necessary to cut through socially acceptable answers to the truth. A celebrated example of indirect techniques was used some years ago in a study of Bowery bums in New York City. A group of sociologists were interviewing a number of these men, and they asked: "Are you married?" They found that an unbelievably large number were not married and never had been. They began to doubt the answers, and wondered whether they were asking the question properly. When they changed the question to read: "Where is your wife?" they got results. The men who had no wives said: "I'm not married," but all the others indirectly admitted that they were. When a man said: "She's in Kalamazoo," the interviewer would check "married."

Mail and Telephone Surveys

The discussion to this point has presumed face-to-face interviews, and such is the recommended practice. Sometimes, however, respondents cannot be seen in person. To interview each member of the sample at home might be prohibitively expensive. In some cases, especially when the polling must be done quickly, there may be too few trained interviewers available, or simply not hours enough to see every respondent in the field. A recent, but unfortunately growing, problem for face-to-face interviewing is the climate of fear and suspicion among Americans. Pollsters report that in many big city apartment areas it is nearly impossible to reach respondents' front doors. Doormen, locked entrance halls, and refusals through apartment squawk-boxes defeat even the most inventive and hardy interviewers. Under such conditions mail or telephone surveys have to be taken.

Mail surveys have two distinct and serious disadvantages. One is that the response to mailed questionnaires is usually much lower than the response to personal interviews. Those who return mail questionnaires (often as low as 10 or 15 percent) are likely to be unrepresentative of the whole universe — but it may be impossible to specify in what ways they differ, or how the responses can be "corrected" by weighting.

Skillful and persevering researchers having respectable scientific or academic auspices can greatly increase the response from mail surveys to the mass public.[17] As would be expected, mail surveys of selected audiences, whose motivation and ability to return are high, usually produce returns of 70 to 90 percent when conducted under prestigious auspices, and when persistent follow-up efforts are made.

The second disadvantage of the mail survey is that it does not allow for quality control of the responses. In the face-to-face situation the interviewer knows that the individual respondent alone gave the answers, and that they were not carelessly or flippantly given (a flippant answer is not necessarily an inaccurate answer, but it often is). A good interviewer can usually prevent unresponsive and manifestly careless answers and will discount, perhaps eliminate, the completed questionnaire of low quality. But there is no such remedy in the mail survey.

A review of the literature (and the wisdom of many years as professional sample designer and teacher of sampling techniques) led Leslie Kish to the following conclusions about the response-rate problem of mail surveys of "literate populations":

1. High responses can be elicited with skillful, brief, simple questionnaires.
2. Three or four mailings will often raise the response to more than 80 or even 90 percent.
3. Interview follow-ups on a subsample of nonresponses will further raise the response rate.

4. Low responses to one or even two mailings should not be accepted, because they often contain severe selection biases.[18]

Telephone surveys carry with them many of the problems of mail surveys — failure to complete the call, high rate of refusals, lack of quality control, danger of interruptions, and/or inattention — and in addition require that the interview schedule be reasonably short. Despite these disadvantages, telephone surveys seem to be more and more used, especially for political or public affairs polling and for follow-up or verification purposes in personal or mail surveys.[19]

The best advice, for the kind of survey research that most social scientists use, is that personal interviewing is much preferred over mail or telephone surveys. Nevertheless, the mail may be used where costs would otherwise be prohibitive, and the telephone can be in many ways a convenient supplement for both personal interviewing and mail questionnaires.

Art and Science in Survey Research

Despite the remarkable growth in both the use and accuracy of public opinion surveys since the middle 1930s, some problems remain. For instance, it is not always certain that the desire for accuracy is foremost in the minds of those who engage pollsters or determine the conditions under which they work. Both the commercial and political results of opinion polling are frequently determined to some extent by the wishes rather than the findings of investigation. The half-truth is more common than either the whole truth or the whole lie.

But to suggest that ethics and motives are unavoidably impure in the use of opinion polling is merely to restate a truism of behavior. A profound truism — and one that is compulsively ignored by utopians of every persuasion — but a truism nevertheless. Polling as a career and as an aid to careers cannot rise above the standards of the other human thoughts and acts to which it is related.

For the purposes of this chapter, however, we have assumed the desire for complete accuracy in opinion measurement. On the purely technical side, we have seen that there are many opportunities for errors in the opinion survey and that the means for eliminating these errors do not exist as yet. We have also seen that the size of the sample is not, generally speaking, a problem in scientific polling. Beyond some fairly small minimum — fifteen hundred or two thousand for a national sample and comparatively fewer, perhaps as few as five hundred, in a smaller universe — the size of the sample does not determine accuracy beyond some usually insignificant degree.

The way the sample is chosen, however, is critical to the accuracy of the survey. So is the way the questions are constructed and ordered in the total questionnaire, the way the interview is carried out in all of its aspects, and the way the responses are subjected to quantitative and qualitative analysis. In all these steps, the artistry of the designer, the interviewer, and the analyst blend with the more mechanical, routine, and uniform elements.[20]

Finally, here is the way a sample was drawn for all adults in the cities of Oakland and Piedmont, California. It is representative of academically sponsored survey research:

A multistage, stratified area sample was used, designed to be approximately self-weighting. The primary sampling units were the 100 census tracts of the two cities. These were divided into three strata by their median monthly rental as reported in the 1960 census. Each stratum was constructed so that it contained almost exactly a third of the population to be studied. Within each stratum, nine census tracts were selected by systematic random sampling with probability proportionate to size. Only 25 tracts, rather than 27, were obtained by this procedure, as two tracts were selected twice.

Enumeration districts were used as the second stage. Two districts were drawn for the two tracts doubly chosen at the first stage, and one district was drawn for each of the remaining tracts. Again, systematic random sampling with probability proportionate to size was employed. A total of 27 enumeration districts resulted.

A team of enumerators was then employed to list all dwelling units in each of the 27 districts. A total of 10,806 dwelling units were found. The 1960 census reported 10,848 units for the same districts. For each district an equal-probability random sample of 22 dwelling units was chosen for interviewing. Units found to be vacant or to have been converted to nonresidential purposes at the time of the field work were replaced by other randomly chosen units.

Within each selected household, an enumeration of all persons over the age of sixteen was made by the interviewer, who then referred to a special table printed on the assignment sheet to select the household member to be interviewed at that address. Eight different sets of tables were used and systematically distributed among the assignment sheets so that the procedure would closely approximate a simple random sampling of the respondents within the household. Thus the interviewer was sent back to the household to obtain an interview with the correct person.[21]

The objective of survey research is to make it possible for more and more aspects of public opinion to be handled mechanically, routinely, and uniformly. In the twenty years between 1933 and 1953,[22] the practitioners of opinion research established their claim, on the basis of this fundamental criterion, to have developed the "scientific measurement of opinion." That the science is by no means complete, and will probably never be complete, makes their achievement not less but more exciting.

Notes:

[1] N. Machiavelli, *The Discourses* (New York: Random House, Inc., Modern Library Edition, 1940), p. 162.

[2] Eugene J. Webb, *et al., Unobtrusive Measures: Nonreactive Research in the Social Sciences* (Chicago: Rand McNally & Company, 1966).

[3] Claude E. Robinson, *Straw Votes: A Study of Political Predicting* (New York: Columbia University Press, 1932), pp. 6-8.

[4] *Ibid.,* p. 9.

[5] *Ibid.,* p. 10.

[6] "Straw Votes," *Encyclopedia of the Social Sciences,* XIV (1937), 417.

[7] John M. Fenton, *In Your Opinion* (Boston: Little, Brown and Company, 1960), p. 3.

[8] "Public Opinion Surveys," *Encyclopaedia Britannica,* XVIII (1955), 744.

[9] Robinson, *op. cit.,* p. 51.

[10] For example, the directors of a survey of American college teachers decided to oversample the large *schools* and at the same time keep their sample of large-college *teachers* in strict proportion to their numbers in the universe. For their procedures in doing this, and for an informative discussion of other sampling techniques used, see Paul F. Lazarsfeld and Wagner Thielens, Jr., *The Academic Mind: Social*

Scientists in a Time of Crisis (New York: The Free Press, 1958), Appendix I, pp. 371-7.

[11] For some insightful comments on the proposition that "the answers pollsters discover are no better than the questions they ask," see Ralph Whitehead, Jr., "Poll Watching: Do We Really Know How the Public Feels About Impeachment?" *Columbia Journalism Review,* XII (March 1974), 3-6.

[12] For an illuminating discussion, with many examples, of the use of small samples, see Hadley Cantril, *Gauging Public Opinion* (Princeton, N.J.: Princeton University Press, 1944), pp. 150-71.

[13] In practice, either the pure random or the stratified-random sample of voters in the state of New Jersey would probably be too expensive, both to select and to interview, and the candidate's pollster would probably sacrifice randomness and use "quota control," or sacrifice state-wide stratification and use geographical area clustering.

[14] Hadley Cantril, "Problems and Techniques: Experiments in the Wording of Questions," *Public Opinion Quarterly,* IV (1940), 67.

[15] Dean D. Knudsen, Hallowell Pope, and Donald P. Irish, "Response Differences to Questions on Sexual Standards: An Interview-Questionnaire Comparison," *Public Opinion Quarterly,* XXXI (1967), 290-7.

[16] For examples and discussion of problems caused by acquiescent and socially acceptable responses, see Richard F. Carter, "Bandwagon and Sandbagging Effects: Some Measures of Dissonance Reduction," *Public Opinion Quarterly,* XXIII (1959), 279-87, and Henry A. Landsberger and Antonio Saavedra, "Response Set in Developing Countries," *Public Opinion Quarterly,* XXXI (1967), 214-29.

[17] See Don A. Dillman, "Increasing Mail Questionnaire Response in Large Samples of the General Public," *Public Opinion Quarterly,* XXXVI (1972), 254-7.

[18] Leslie Kish, *Survey Sampling* (New York: John Wiley & Sons, Inc., 1965), pp. 538-9. For a good general discussion of return-rate problems and devices for dealing with them, see William J. Crotty, "The Utilization of Mail Questionnaires and the Problem of a Representative Return Rate," *Western Political Quarterly,* XIX (1966), 44-53.

[19] Joseph E. Bachelder, Nixon's pollster in the 1968 campaign, was reported as saying that the Texas Poll once took simultaneous statewide telephone and personal-interview surveys and found no significant difference (*New York Times,* July 15, 1968). Daniel Yankelovich, the 1972 pollster for the *New York Times,* used telephone interviews

exclusively in 16 key electoral states, polling in at least four waves from July 24 to October 24. The representativeness and validity of his responses cannot be judged from the *Times* reports, but it seems that he accurately captured the major developments and shifts of opinion in the lopsided contest of that year.

[20] For data analysis, undergraduates may find helpful relevant chapters in Earl R. Babbie, *Survey Research Methods* (Belmont, Calif.: Wadsworth Publishing Co., 1973). The re-analysis of survey data obtained from repositories is also increasingly possible for graduate students and the more serious undergraduates: See Herbert H. Hyman, *Secondary Analysis of Sample Surveys: Principles, Procedures, and Potentialities* (New York: John Wiley & Sons, Inc., 1972).

[21] Charles Y. Glock, Gertrude J. Selznick, and Joe L. Spaeth, *The Apathetic Majority: A Study Based on Public Responses to the Eichmann Trial* (New York: Harper & Row, Inc., 1966), pp. 183-4. Reprinted by permission of Harper & Row.

[22] Neither 1933 nor 1953 stands out in the history of opinion polling with any commanding claim as era markers — as the dates of great discoveries or publications are (with some dubious simplicity) said to be. The first may fairly represent the time in which the marriage of mathematics and social psychology produced one of its most valuable offspring, the scientific sampling of human populations. The second marks the time in which the figurative child of this marriage reached its majority after an adolescence filled with many "crises of identity," of which the 1948 election was the most traumatic.

3 What Opinions Mean

Public opinion polling is, by now, an accepted and regular part of political life in America. The political and governmental applications of survey research are so widespread and so valuable for candidates, policy-makers, and administrators that it would be unthinkable to do without them.

The attacks on polling and pollsters are of two kinds, mainly. One claims that survey research as applied to politics is so inaccurate that it is worth very little as a measurement of the voters' real policy views or candidate preferences. That argument says, in effect, that there are so many sources of error that one can't trust the findings of pollsters.

The other main criticism of political polling says that it is injurious to democracy. It declares that evil and injury to democracy would follow if the pollsters did what they claim to do; accurate and reliable polling, these critics assert, would be a disservice to democracy.

The two arguments are surely different and may not be logically consistent. Those who make the dangers-to-democracy argument at least implicitly say polling is accurate, for if the polls were truly such inaccurate measures as the first critics claim, then they presumably would not be used and would not injure democracy. But it might be countered that political polls are both inaccurate and dangerous to democracy precisely because citizens and politicians, not aware of their inaccuracies, place unwarranted faith in them. The two criticisms of polling are not separable in reality, then, and the arguments will necessarily overlap.

METHODOLOGY: INACCURACIES

Probably the most common complaint against the pollsters is that they do not achieve representative cross sections of the universe whose opinions they aspire to measure. Beyond the points made in the last chapter, only two more need be made here.

The first is less general and refers to the measurement of opinions and the prediction of behavior from *subsamples*. Because of the operation of the electoral college, presidential elections depend on a candidate's getting a plurality of votes in states that together produce a majority of electoral votes. A national poll that forecasts a country-wide popular vote for a candidate is therefore no predictor of success in a close race. Ideally, candidates need to know how they are doing in each state, or at least in those major states that can produce an electoral college majority.

Bear in mind that very small samples are unreliable. Cantril indicates that two hundred are about minimum for any useful sample, and that samples of fewer than fifty are not worth experimenting with, while Yankelovich testified in 1972 that at least 250 interviews are necessary to obtain a 6 percent sampling error within a state.[1]

Despite this requirement the pollsters have reported their results for individual or important states during presidential campaigns. If we make the unrealistic assumption that the respondents in a sample of two thousand are distributed throughout all fifty states according to the population of each state, the prediction for a state of seven million would have to be based on a sample of seventy-seven interviews, for a state of three million on thirty-three interviews, and Nevada's prediction on the basis of a sample of two voters. This breakdown, of course, is a reductio ad absurdum; but it illustrates the impossibility of predicting state votes from subcells of national samples. The importance of the electoral-college system to the presidential race, however, makes it imperative to consider state-by-state forecasts, and the pollsters continue to do so.

The second point about sample size is only to suggest that techniques are well known and available for creating samples that, within rather small limits, closely resemble the universe from which they are drawn. If not all the pollsters use these techniques — and some do not — those who have the responsibility for such surveys and those who use the results are obliged to assess for themselves and their readers what the consequences of their technological imperfections may be. Some polling for commercial purposes — and perhaps even for political purposes — may quite honestly be done with less than the best techniques, when, for reasons of cost or time, no better can be employed. But in such cases the procedures and probable errors should always be described when the results are used.

Fairness requires not only that the pollsters describe their sample design and actual sample but that they describe the analytical assumptions and devices on which their reports or conclusions are based. For instance, the handling of the "don't know" responses has always been a source of disagreement among pollsters and of confusion among laymen. The "don't know" dilemma is one of the unsolved problems about which pollsters ought to be quite candid — and for which, if they are not candid, they deserve to be rebuked.

In pre-election polls of the who-do-you-intend-to-vote-for-variety, a "don't know" is reported as "undecided." The terms are used interchangeably, but the problem of interpretation does not therefore disappear. Are the "undecideds" truly undecided or just indifferent? If they are indifferent, most of them probably will not vote at all; if those who vote divide between the candidates, the category can be ignored. It is likely, however, that those who are indifferent yet actually vote will choose the candidates favored by their friends, their neighbors, or their socioeconomic class; through the use of such indices, an intelligent prediction may be made of the distribution of these votes. The ultimate choice of the true undecided may likewise be predicted by the use of *expected correlations* between individual behavior and socioeconomic factors; but it may be necessary, in addition, to look for idiosyncratic clues in each questionnaire. However the undecideds are handled, the pollsters have an obligation to disclose — and the readers have a right to know — the process by which the analysis was made.

The practical difficulties of this kind of reporting, however, are apparent. Discussions of assumptions and explanations of procedures are apt to be too dry, technical, and uninteresting to be included in news stories. The requirements of crisp reporting and of analytical exactness may be incompatible. Normal newspaper reporting of public opinion measurement cannot be expected to meet the ideal requisites of social science research, although conscientious journalism might make more use of feature stories and expert critiques in reporting poll data.

Some critics of modern polling point out that the "don't know" categories, aside from being inadequately interpreted, are generally underestimated. A number of reasons are advanced to explain this underestimation. For one, it is argued that the structure of the questionnaire and the sociopsychological pressures of the interview situation account together for a serious error in measuring "real" opinion. However, it is unavoidable that brief and somewhat superficial interviews of the kind done by pollsters must be structured to some considerable degree. Questions are often of the dichotomous or cafeteria sort, and the respondent finds it easy to give definite rather than "don't know" answers. In most cases, he does so without any danger of being exposed by later questions, even when he does not have any opinion. The use of two-step or other screening questions has been recommended to filter out the "knows" from the "don't knows."

DO THEY TELL THE TRUTH?

This brief consideration of the problems of measuring "don't knows" leads readily into a different but related criticism of the pollsters. It has been said that respondents will not give honest answers to many of the questions asked in opinion surveys. Lindsay Rogers, whose dyspeptic book *The Pollsters* is one of the most celebrated attacks on opinion measurements, wonders whether "public opinion is ever the sum of the answers that people are willing to give to strangers," and quotes the view of the director of Mass Observation that "*public opinion is what you say out loud to anyone*. It is an overt and not necessarily candid part of your private opinion."[2]

Indications are that a considerable number of people incorrectly answer even factual questions for which the truth can be checked from public records. One study of 920 Denver adults in early 1949 found invalidity in one-seventh to one-fourth of the answers to questions about voting in six earlier elections. Thirteen percent of the respondents who said they had voted in the November 1948 presidential election actually had not.[3]

It is not surprising, perhaps, that respondents will lie about facts of behavior when the truth is ego-damaging; but in the Denver study, 10 percent of the respondents claimed to have valid drivers' licenses and had not, 9 percent said they had public library cards and had not, 3 percent claimed to own automobiles and did not, and 3 percent claimed to own their homes and did not.

There appears to be a hard core of liars on even the most socially neutral questions — a group that is joined by many as the questions become increasingly ego-related. This matter demands the practiced judgment of the conscientious poll taker and analyst; estimates of the importance of distortion and what can be done about it have to be made for each case on its own conditions.

It is equally impossible to generalize, at this stage in the development of opinion measurement, about the effects of strangers as interviewers. The implication in Rogers' criticism is that people are more apt to tell the truth to their friends than to strangers. The answer to this implication is yes and no. A number of psychological theories suggest (and interviewing experience attests) the notion that some kinds of people will be more candid about some things with strangers than with friends. All interviewers have heard truths from respondents who would under no conditions tell them to friends or neighbors. And it may be — although it has not been proved, or even tested, to my knowledge — that opinions on political issues are more freely given to strangers. A case can be made that the impersonal stranger, once established in the respondent's eyes as a reputable fact gatherer, is more apt to be trusted with confidence than is someone the respondent must see on a day-to-day basis. One hundred and forty years ago de Tocqueville observed that "A stranger frequently hears important truths at the fireside of his host, which the latter would perhaps conceal from the ear of friendship; he consoles himself with his guest for the silence to which he is restricted, and the shortness of the traveller's stay takes away all fear of his indiscretion."[4]

VALIDITY AND RELIABILITY

Validity in polling has to do with whether the respondent's real opinion is discovered. But, strange as it may seem, for some purposes and under some circumstances it may not matter whether real opinion is revealed. Although the psychologist may be concerned with the correspondence between private opinion (what the individual *really* thinks) and public opinion (what he *says* he thinks), the political sociologist is primarily interested in the correspondence between the individual's public opinion and his related behavior. If the individual supports Candidate X in pre-election polls and votes for Candidate X in the election, it is, for most political analyses, irrelevant whether or not he really prefers Candidate X. Although the reasons for liking or disliking a policy or a candidate are important for strategic purposes — and tests of logic and relevancy may be necessary for certain kinds of analyses — the first practical test for the political meaning of public opinion is not the ultimate truthfulness of inner conviction but the internal consistency of public behavior.

To the political scientist, *reliability* is probably more important than validity. Reliability is judged by the reproducibility of a measurement result. A testing technique is said to have high reliability when it consistently measures the same dimensions with similar results.

A poll may be valid for aggregate purposes even if there are many invalid individual responses. Of a California sample 24 percent misrepresented their voter registration status (most seemed to be lying in response to the social desirability tendency). But they were so consistently untruthful that for predictive purposes the lack of validity of individual responses would not have reduced the validity of the whole survey.

> While those who lied about registering also lied about voting, their lies so faithfully mirrored the responses of genuine voters that their inclusion in the sample would lead to a "prediction" *in this instance* that was substantially as accurate as one from the . . . known registrants.[5]

An early test of poll reliability used gross national survey data gathered over several years. Using results of comparable studies and questions of four independent polling organizations the most general and significant finding involved a set of ninety-nine pairs of questions in which the average difference was 3.24 percentage points.[6]

Opinion pollsters like the chance to forecast elections. Elections constitute one of the rare means for checking poll results — perhaps the only regular and systematic test that is not experimentally staged or based on a number of demographic and sociological assumptions. The "givens" in an election are regularized, anticipated, and (aside from possible bandwagon effect) beyond the influence of the pollster.

The margin of error between the predicted popular vote and the actual vote for a candidate is a rough test of the validity of the prediction for that election. For a number of elections, these errors may be taken collectively as a gross estimation of poll validity. Similarly, the differences between or among poll forecasts for the same political race constitute a test of reliability. When aggregated, they may give us clues as to the general reliability of polls.

The average error for all 245 national, sectional, state, and local election predictions made by the Gallup Poll from 1936 to 1950 was four percentage points.[7] Since 1948, however, Gallup and the other major political pollsters have vastly improved their polling techniques and their understanding about political behavior. In six presidential and congressional elections, 1950 through 1960, the Gallup agency averaged an error of *less than 1 percent.*[8] Gallup's error in 1964 was 2.6 percent; in 1968 it was only 0.4 percent, and in 1972 it was 0.2 percent.

MEASUREMENT OF THE INTENSITY OF OPINION

It is charged, finally, that the polls distort the "truth" about public opinion because they do not measure the intensity of opinions. With regard to the intensity of opinion we ask ourselves when and under what conditions we care how strongly people hold their opinions. Intensity is important to the extent that there is a public issue that is expected soon to be settled by election or action of a representative body, where individuals are free to participate according to how strongly they feel, and where intensity therefore has predictive value for estimating the outcome of the settlement. Some examples may be helpful.

If a poll is taken on the same day as the election to which it is related (an unlikely exercise), intensity of opinion is not an important element. The reason is that in the election each vote is equal to every other vote, no matter how intensely the voters feel about the election — and on election day we may assume it is too late for voters who feel intensely about the election to influence the opinions of voters who do not feel intensely about it. On the other hand, whenever there is an opportunity for persons who feel intensely about an issue to influence the opinions of those who do not feel strongly, then the strength of opinions is important for meaningful measurement if any prediction is being attempted.

In order to deal more satisfactorily with intensity of opinion, it may be helpful to introduce the concept of *distribution* of opinion. On any issue, the range of possible opinion may be described as from "strongly favor" to "strongly oppose"; conceptually, we imagine a continuum of opinions with each person falling on the scale somewhere between the two ends, "strongly favor" and "strongly oppose." In practice, question construction results in opinions being grouped into three ("favor," "neutral," "oppose") or five positions ("strongly favor," "favor," "neutral," "oppose," "strongly oppose"). So arranged (as continua, or in scales, showing both direction and intensity), opinion distribution may be said to have two basic forms: consensual patterns and conflict patterns.

The late V. O. Key, Jr., described as a "supportive consensus" the situation in which opinion underpins existing policy and practice.[9] A supportive consensus distribution is shown in Figure 3-1.

A "permissive consensus," as shown in Figure 3-2, is one that allows but does not actively support a policy (a policy here to mean an official, or governmental, position on an issue).

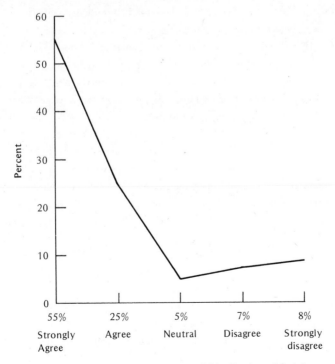

FIGURE 3-1.   A "Supportive Consensus" Distribution of Opinion

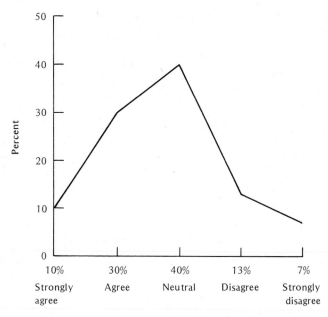

FIGURE 3-2.   A "Permissive Consensus" Distribution of Opinion

Conflict distributions of public opinion may be bimodal or multi-modal, but the two most common seem to be those in which opinion is quite sharply polarized with few neutrals, and those in which there are opposing groups with strong feelings but also a relatively large indifferent middle, as shown in Figures 3-3 and 3-4.

Do the pollsters give sufficient attention to intensity of opinions? Like most other persons, pollsters seem to know better than they do. During a campaign, the journalistic pressures and the pressures from the clamoring players of the great game of politics seem to prevent the application of the most refined (which are usually the most costly and almost always the slowest) research tools. The headlines seem inevitably to make their own conditions when attention is focused on political opinions; qualifications of findings, scales of pluses and minuses, and rows of gray figures without clear winners and losers do not appeal to the consuming public in periods of high political fever. But when political fever gives way to the other fevers recorded by the mass media, who then will pay for the energies of Gallup's nine hundred interviewers, the analysts, and the machine time to consider carefully the intensity with which pro-McGovern voters liked McGovern (or disliked Nixon), or

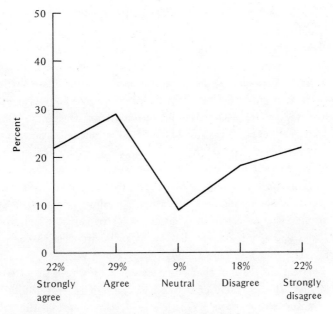

FIGURE 3-3. Bimodal Conflict Distribution of Opinion

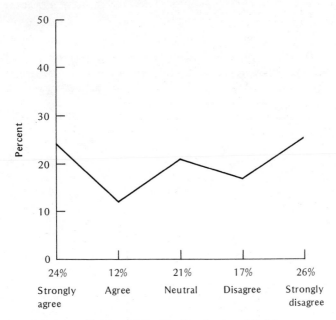

FIGURE 3-4. Multimodal Conflict Distribution of Opinion

whether the "no" received in answer to the question "Do you favor federal aid to education?" was really "I guess not" or "Hell, no!"

When seen in this light, this criticism becomes much like the other procedural charges made against pollsters. The pollsters, when they are able to resist economic and journalistic pressures, are aware that they do not have magical devices with which they can accurately map, like aerial photographers, each ridge and furrow of public opinion. Nor do they believe — even though in fanciful and unguarded moments they may seem to believe — that they can perfect democracy singlehandedly if the rest of us will just have faith in them. On the whole, it is unfair to charge them with such vanities. What they may fairly be charged with, as the most sensitive among them will agree, is a failure to explain at every opportunity and in as much detail as the given situation permits the limitations and qualifications that ought to be attached to every poll result.[10] They ought to report modestly and conservatively and to stress much more than they do that every statement described as a "result" or "finding" is not a fact but an approximation of a fact. Possibly, ultimate candor ought to move them to say something like this at the beginning of each poll release: "We have been as careful as possible to keep errors out of our work, but we know the chances are that the following approximations are wrong by as much as 3 to 4 percent (or perhaps even more, depending on the ways in which some people would have us calculate the error). Still, experience indicates that the methods we have used in obtaining these careful guesses about public opinion are better than any other methods that we know. Here, then, are the results of our measurements. . . ."[11]

POLITICAL POLLING:
HOW MUCH, BY WHOM, AND SO WHAT?

Polling enthusiasts are fond of quoting the English nobleman James Bryce on the nature of public opinion in a democratic society. In 1888 Lord Bryce suggested that there had been, by that time, three identifiable stages in the development of public opinion, and that

A fourth stage would be reached if the will of the majority of the citizens were to become ascertainable at all times, and without the need of its passing through a body of representatives, possibly even without the need of voting machinery at all.

Popular government would have been pushed so far as almost to dispense with, or at any rate to anticipate, the legal modes in which the majority speaks its will at the polling booths; and this informal but direct control of the multitude would dwarf, if it did not supersede the importance of those formal but occasional deliverances made at the elections of representatives. To such a condition of things the phrase "Rule of public opinion" might be most properly applied, for public opinion would not only reign but govern.[12]

Like Bryce's "fourth stage," the opinion-policy process in direct democracy presumes that popular opinion is turned directly into governmental policy. When sampling techniques become perfect (or nearly perfect) — or so the argument goes — opinion polling will be equal to referenda. Instead of all the people making policy, as in a plebiscite, a perfectly representative sample can do so; thereupon, legislatures may be reduced to rule-making and constituency-service agencies — or, ultimately, abolished. Such a system, while as yet practically unattainable, has a certain superficial appeal in theory.

We may call this kind of direct democracy *opinion-sample majoritarianism,* to distinguish it from the face-to-face majoritarianism of town-meeting democracy. No pollster has ever quite declared that majority opinion, as measured by sample surveys, ought to be translated directly into policy. But some pollsters have implied that opinion-sample majoritarians might be found among them if the necessary opinion-measuring machinery could be created.

At the opposite extreme from direct majoritarians are avowed minoritarians, who believe that policy ought to reflect the views of elite groups who for special reasons of birth, wealth, intellect, or tradition are "fit" to govern the masses. To minoritarians, the opinions of large publics are of no concern, except as they may be manipulated by "superior" groups in the struggle to control governmental policy.

Although we should not ignore the dangers to democracy of both right- and left-wing minoritarianism, we need do no more at this point than to note the existence of such views, and to suggest that the relationship of public opinion to minoritarian government is quite simple: If public opinion does not threaten the government, it is ignored; if it threatens the government, it is corrected; if it supports the government, it is patronized and rewarded.

Qualified Majoritarianism and Public Opinion Polling

For our understanding of the meaning of public opinion in democracy, the important spectrum of beliefs on the majority-minority continuum may be called *qualified majoritarianism*. One kind of qualified majoritarianism is *coalition majoritarianism*. Although it is something of an oversimplification, we may say that the United States national government, in theory and in practice, observes coalition majoritarianism. Within a complex and highly fractionalized governmental framework of federalism and separation of powers, policy is made by temporary and ad hoc coalitions of groups and individuals. There is a presumption – although it is only a presumption, because the reality is immeasurable – that a popular majority (or something near it) is represented by the coalitions that are successful in making policy on particular issues. Under these conditions, the opinion-policy process is very much like that described on pages 16-20 above. When policy is made by coalition majorities in the United States, the coalitions do not consist of internally disciplined parties, as is usually the case in Continental Europe, but of political individuals and groups (including party groups) with various strengths, goals, and access to the decision-making process.

Public Opinion Polling and Mixed Democracy

Among believers in the American system of mixed democracy (or coalition majoritarianism), there are both agreement and disagreement about the place and the significance of public opinion polling. After thirty years of agitation and controversy, it appears that pollsters and critics agree that most public opinion polling serves some intelligence function for policymakers – it gives them information that may influence their understanding or beliefs – and that skillful polling may give them certain kinds of information that cannot be obtained in any other way.

Beyond this, however, agreement is less frequent, and conflicting points of view are more common. One critic argues that the activities of pollsters – especially the way they report their findings and the way these findings are accepted (interpreted) by newspaper-reading Americans – constitute a "disservice to democracy." The essence of democracy, according to John C. Ranney, lies in an endless discussion of issues and policies. Such a dynamic, ever-changing, and always open dialogue among individuals and groups is, as we have seen, the heart of the opinion-policy process. Ranney declares that the danger in public opinion polls is that the participants in this critical dialogue may take the polls to be more important than they are.[13] To the degree that poll results are assumed to be the last and, in a sense, authoritative word on any public issue, to that extent the opinion-policy process becomes slowed, rigid, and inoperative — and, to that extent, democracy has been ill served.

There is little evidence, however, to indicate that poll reports have significantly slowed or interfered with the opinion-policy process. It may be partly a result of the limits and inherent errors in polling — demonstrated from time to time (as in 1948) and admitted by the more careful pollsters — that the published results of polls have not noticeably rigidified the opinion-policy process. So many elections are determined within the 6 percent range that pollsters allow themselves for error, and so many issues depend on the unpollable factors in the opinion-policy process, that the participants in the dialogue have found that poll results cannot be the sole or even the major determinant of their behavior. If the pollsters could claim 100 percent, or near 100 percent, accuracy, their pronouncements might have the result that Ranney fears. But as long as their admitted margin of error is greater than the margin that usually determines the important elections, there seems no likelihood that the political controversy upon which democracy depends will be stopped or even appreciably slowed.

Although this speculative danger does not seem to be imminent, Ranney at least implies that perfect measurement of public opinion would be a disservice, because cross-sectional readings of the opinion of the moment would be substituted for an understanding of the opinion-policy process as a dynamic, never-ending phenomenon. This is a profound and stimulating criticism, and one upon which it is not too extreme to say that those who understand democracy can be separated from those who do not.

If all opinion could be known at any given moment, this measurement would not, except in the most doctrinaire and theoretical sense of majority rule, be the sole basis for policymaking. Despite the way pollsters used to talk, no one believes that other factors should be excluded from policymaking. Above all else, policymakers have to be prospective. They must think about tomorrow. Aside from the possibility that opinion may be wrong, nothing is more certain than that opinion will change. Decisions must be made on many grounds, involving many facts, judgments, and plain old hunches. In one profound sense, what the people think today is not so important to political actors as what the people will think tomorrow, especially if tomorrow happens to be election day. The politician who takes the momentary measurement of opinion — however accurate — as the sole criterion for decisionmaking is not only unfit for public office in a democracy, but, from the point of view of a political career, an ignoramus. If the perfect measurement of opinion had the effect of making large numbers of policymakers follow public opinion slavishly, democracy would indeed suffer a disservice. It is hard to believe, however, that even perfect measurement would induce any number of political actors to be so simpleminded in their understanding of the opinion-policy process.

What if the belief, or fact, of perfect measurement encourages the *electorate* to reduce the amount of testing, weighing, and discussion of public policy? If this occurred, we could again agree with Ranney that the polls would be doing a disservice to democracy. But it seems no more probable that knowing what people think today will determine what people will think tomorrow than that it will determine what decisionmakers decide today. The political nonelites are, after all, influenced by public officials and other opinion leaders, just as the reverse is true. The opinion-policy process is a two-way street, and as long as significant numbers of the public recognize the complex nature of this interplay there would seem to be little danger that the political dialogue will be slowed or ended. The leaders of interest groups will continue to attempt to influence opinion no matter how accurately it is measured. Some individuals and groups seem, in fact, to be more vigorous when they suspect themselves to be in the minority. Those who enjoy majority support know that when the count is taken again their happy position may be reversed or weakened unless they continue to promote the democratic dialogue. Hardening of the arteries of public controversy is not likely to take place, regardless of polling accuracy. I think it is safe to assert that the dangers Ranney envisioned nearly thirty years ago are now no more likely to take place than are the early pollsters' vastly more simple notions that polling heralded the last and perfect stage of democracy.

Name Familiarity and Bandwagon

You will not be surprised to hear that most of the practicing politicians who criticize polling are those whom the polls show to be running behind. We assume, therefore, that much of their criticism is self-serving, and is best understood as part of campaign rhetoric, as part of the charges and countercharges of electioneering. Candidates who attack opinion polls because the polls show them to have less support than their opponents tend to focus on the motivations and integrity of the pollsters as well as on the accuracy of the polls. Thus Governor Wallace in 1968 charged that the two major-party candidates and the national pollsters had rigged the results against him.[14] In 1972 the McGovern supporters and the candidate himself characterized poll releases during the campaign as "propaganda that the Democratic Party can't win," "another wrong and inaccurate piece of information"; and on the day before the elections McGovern said with regard to the last poll, "It's nuts."[15]

More serious than the carping of losing candidates is the misleading effect of name familiarity. The argument here is simply that respondents often give preference early in the campaign to potential candidates merely because they know who these individuals are.

Then-Senator Albert Gore (D—Tenn.) raised the question of name familiarity in a dramatic way during a hearing in early 1960.[16] To test his view that name familiarity has an effect on pre-election responses (he need not have bothered — the literature is full of evidence that it does), in early 1960 he had his office staff poll 182 residents of Washington, D.C., using "an exact duplicate of Dr. Gallup's poll card except that we supplied the names of the persons on the card." The names on the Democratic card were:

1. Allen Dulles
2. John D. Eisenhower
3. Hubert Humphrey
4. Lyndon Johnson
5. Thomas Jefferson Jones
6. John F. Kennedy
7. Franklin D. Roosevelt, Jr.
8. Adlai Stevenson
9. Stuart Symington

Of the 120 respondents who took the Democratic card, Senator Gore reported that "25 percent listed either Franklin D. Roosevelt, Jr., or John D. Eisenhower as their preference for either first or second choice." Though neither of these persons was a potential candidate, one-quarter of the respondents chose them over others who were announced or publicly assumed to be candidates.

Senator Gore queried both Gallup and Roper on, among other things, their views of the effects of name familiarity in pre-election polls. The question was: "Do you consider a poll on presidential candidates a measure of popular support? Or, in your opinion, is it a reflection of familiarity with a name or names, or is it a favorable or unfavorable reaction to a name or names?"

Gallup's reply was equivocal, but Roper candidly replied that early poll results are "certainly much more a reflection of familiarity with names than anything else — until after the campaign itself has started." "In a sense," Mr. Roper declared,

I share *some* of Senator Gore's misgivings, particularly about the effect of the polls on *nominations.* I have been dismayed to find many convention delegates exhibiting an obsessive and exclusive interest in finding a winner, dismayed at the weight given to preconvention polls, which are in my opinion little more than a name-familiarity game, but which are often accepted as gospel evidence of the ability to win in November.[17]

Roper's sensitivity to the effect of name familiarity is further revealed by his comments about the timing of pre-election polls (and, incidentally, in his disclosure that the demands of the mass media may intensify the unfortunate effects of name familiarity):

We do not customarily start doing any research having to do with any aspect of the election until sometime during the year in which the election is to be held, and then we put more effort on trying to find out what might be described as the "general mood" of the people than we do on the "popularity contest" aspect of it — although naturally, in order to get any newspapers or television networks to sponsor us, we have to pay some attention to that.[18]

Whether polling helps create a "bandwagon effect" in a campaign is an old and much discussed question. The bandwagon argument says that undecided and apolitical voters tend to support an apparent victor simply because he is an apparent victor. People, it is said, like to back a winner.

There is little evidence that a bandwagon effect occurs. In the first place, the logic of the argument is not persuasive. People like to back a winner in matters to which they attach importance. But the bandwagon argument supposes that the voter is indifferent to the outcome. It could be said then, that the effect cannot occur, by definition, either to the indifferent or to the concerned voter. If the voter is indifferent, he will not care who wins or whom he votes for — nor will he, at the moment of voting, have any memory of poll predictions; on the other hand, if he favors Candidate A, he is not apt to vote for B simply because a poll predicted B's election.

Beyond this argument, which is something of a logical quibble, it is not at all clear that public faith in the pollsters is high enough after 1948, despite the good showings of the 1960s, to warrant wide adoption of a bandwagon psychology. Roper's comment on possible bandwagon effect merits attention:

> I don't think there is much evidence that the polls directly influence the voters' preferences. If there were a "bandwagon effect," it seems to me that polls would always underpredict the margin of victory, since the whole theory of bandwagon is that more and more people jump on it, and there just has to be a week between the last poll and election day. As a matter of fact, surveys have overpredicted the margin of the winner at least as much as they have underpredicted it.[19]

In response to the criticisms of political polling, the profession recently adopted some principles of recommended practice. During the presidential campaign of 1968 the Standards Committee of the American Association for Public Opinion Research recommended that pollsters include in any news release essentials of the survey methodology, and inform their private clients *in detail* of the elements of the research design. Their "minimal disclosure" standards for news releases are worth listing here in full:

1. Identity of who *sponsored* the survey.
2. The *exact wording* of questions asked.
3. A *definition of the population* actually sampled.
4. *Size of Sample.* For mail surveys, this should include both the number of questionnaires mailed out and the number returned.
5. An indication of what allowance should be made for *sampling error.*
6. *Which results are based on parts of the sample*, rather than the total sample. (For example: likely voters only, those aware of an event, those who answered other questions in a certain way.)
7. *Whether interviewing was done personally*, by telephone, mail, or on street corners.
8. *Timing* of the interviewing in relation to relevant events.[20]

The Standards Committee "strongly urged" the news media to ask for and include all the above in their final copy for public polls and for private polls the results of which are made public. The typical releases of Gallup, Harris, and other major pollsters carried more of the recommended information after the action of the AAPOR Committee; many smaller and private pollsters continue to release "findings" without sufficient information for judging validity.

Congressman Lucien Nedzi (D–Mich.) would go further. He introduced a bill in 1968 that would require disclosure of Items 1, 2, 4, 7, and 8 above for any newspaper-published poll. Paralleling Items 3 and 5, the Nedzi bill would disclose "the method used in compiling the sample," "the number in the sample who were contacted and responded, the number in the sample who were contacted and did not respond, and the number in the sample who were not contacted."[21]

Opinion Polling by Political Leaders

We have seen that political leaders in a democracy must give unflagging attention to opinion measurement. Though often valid, the "horseback" judgments of even the most seasoned politicians cannot match the reliability of scientific surveys. As opinion polling has gained greater respectability, and a body of basic theory and technical skill, even the older politicians have accepted — often reluctantly — this new technique.

There is, of course, a certain amount of so-called polling that is faked, wholly or in part, with the predetermined results eagerly taken and printed by a gullible press. This is all in the tradition of fairness in love, war, and politics, and may even be a matter of pride in an age of "dirty tricks."

But since the early 1950s honest polls are increasingly used by candidates at all levels. Great amounts of campaign money are available in presidential years, and polls are among the frills that, through a cooperative trickle-down process, candidates for lesser offices may share. Governors, senators, state party leaders, and even city and county candidates often commission their own polls nowadays. When William Scranton finished his term as Governor of Pennsylvania he took away five cartons (each 12 by 15 by 10 inches) of polls that had been done for him by professional John Bucci between 1961 and 1967.[22]

The amount of material — guides, handbooks, campaign managers' instructions — now emerging from the national party committees and the larger state committees is convincing evidence that the volume and the quality of political opinion research is already high and still growing.[23] In 1972 a data-processing firm collected the names of 1.5 million Democratic and independent voters in Ohio, arranging them geographically by education, union membership, religion, home ownership, age, and income level; the Ohio Democratic Party, which paid $250,000 for the service, could then make highly specialized appeals to subgroups of potential supporters, and could engage in the most finely tuned opinion research.[24] As early as 1960 the Kennedy presidential campaign used trend data and aggregated poll responses to predict voter behavior; data from 66 surveys, representing a total of more than 130,000 interviews from 1952 to 1959, were fed into the computers in developing the Kennedy strategy.[25]

Other computer operations use data from bellwether or swing-voting constituencies to give a basis for early prediction of winners after the votes from only a few such districts are counted. In the critical California Republican primary of 1964, CBS predicted Senator Goldwater's victory on the basis of just 42 of the more than 32,000 precincts in that state, and before the polls were closed in some other precincts.

Many political leaders and others concerned with the protection of voting rights and procedures saw dangers in the possibility of computer prediction of election winners before all voters had cast their ballots. Some critics argued that people would be discouraged from voting if the results could be more or less confidently known before the polls were closed. Others agreed that a bandwagon effect would occur in the last minutes of voting as persons switched to the apparent winner. One senator proposed a bill to outlaw the broadcast of both returns and predictions until all polls had closed in the United States. Other senators moved to establish a uniform closing time for federal elections — one version would close the polls at 11 P.M. in the Eastern time zone and at 5 P.M. in the Bering time zone (the farthest west zone of the Alaska islands) — but so far no legislation has been passed.

Research has not discovered significant effects of early predictions on either turnout or candidate choice in the western states. The most recent published study (of the 1968 election) concludes in this way:

. . . Of the four major studies conducted to determine possible effects of election night broadcasts on the 1964 presidential election, none detected measurable effects on voting behavior. These studies indicated that the broadcasts had no detectable influence on voting behavior in a landslide election in which the results were also anticipated well in advance of the election itself. The present study covers the case of a close election in which the closeness of the contest was also anticipated and further reflected in the early returns and projections on the broadcasts themselves. In this type of situation, too, there were no detectable effects.[26]

Notes:

[1] Hadley Cantril *et al., Gauging Public Opinion* (Princeton, N.J.: Princeton University Press, 1944), pp. 130-1, 150-71, and 298, and *Public Opinion Polls: Hearings Before the Subcommittee on Library and Memorials of the Committee on House Administration,* Ninety-third Congress, First Session, September 19-21 and October 5, 1972, p. 247.

[2] Lindsay Rogers, *The Pollsters* (New York: Alfred A. Knopf, Inc., 1949), pp. 37, 41-2. Italics in original.

[3] Hugh J. Parry and Helen M. Crossley, "Validity of Responses to Survey Questions," *Public Opinion Quarterly,* XIV (1950), 397. Clausen estimated that 7 percent of the 1964 SRC national survey respondents lied about voting. – Aage R. Clausen, "Response Validity: Vote Report," *Public Opinion Quarterly,* XXXII (1968-69), 588-606. Gabriel reports that in his Rhode Island interviews "many lied in claiming to have voted." – Richard A. Gabriel, "A New Theory of Ethnic Voting," *Polity,* IV (1972), 414. My students in Santa Clara County, California, discovered that 9 percent of their respondents lied about voting in 1974.

[4] Alexis de Tocqueville, *Democracy in America* (London: Oxford University Press, 1946 ed.), Author's Preface to the First Part, p. 17.

[5] Charles G. Bell and William Buchanan, "Reliable and Unreliable Respondents: Party Registration and Prestige Pressure," *The Western Political Quarterly,* XIX (1966), 43. Italics in the original.

[6] Hadley Cantril, "Do Different Polls Get the Same Results?" *Public Opinion Quarterly,* IX (1945), 62.

[7] George Gallup, "The Gallup Poll and the 1950 Election," *Public Opinion Quarterly,* XV (1951), 21.

[8] Paul Perry, "Election Survey Procedures of the Gallup Poll," *Public Opinion Quarterly,* XXIV (1960), 531-42; and, by the same author

(who is president of the Gallup Organization, Inc.), "Gallup Poll Election Survey Experience, 1950 to 1960," *Public Opinion Quarterly,* XXVI (1962), 272-9.

[9] Key's discussion of the distribution of opinions — both distribution of intensity and geographical distribution of intensity in America — is the best in the literature, and I am indebted to his work for many of the ideas and for some of the language of this section. See V. O. Key, Jr., *Public Opinion and American Democracy* (New York: Alfred A. Knopf, Inc., 1961), Chapters 2-5.

[10] After reviewing all schedules and other analytical materials used by three research groups in a study of social scientists teaching in United States colleges, David Riesman concluded "that roughly 10 percent of the interviews misfired in some decisive fashion." — "Some Observations on the Interviewing," in Paul F. Lazarsfeld and Wagner Thielens, Jr., *The Academic Mind* (New York: The Free Press, 1958), p. 271. Since the study that Riesman reviewed was a model of care and precision, we may assume that 10 percent is something like a minimum for interviewing error — that at least one of ten interviews "misfires in some decisive fashion." However, this assumption does not mean that the accumulated quantitative results are 10 percent in error, for many of the errors cancel out in the summing.

[11] See p. 71 for the recommended "minimal disclosure" standards of the American Association for Public Opinion Research.

[12] *The American Commonwealth, Vol. II* (London: Macmillan & Co., Ltd., 1888), p. 220-1.

[13] John C. Ranney, "Do the Polls Serve Democracy?" *Public Opinion Quarterly,* X (1946), 349-60.

[14] *New York Times,* October 11, 1968.

[15] Robert H. Blank, "Published Opinion Polls and the Conduct of the 1972 Presidential Campaign" (Paper delivered at the Western Political Science Association Meeting, San Diego, California, April 7, 1973).

[16] *Congressional Record* (February 11, 1960), p. 2,203-6. See also Charles W. Roll, Jr., and Albert H. Cantril, *Polls: Their Use and Misuse in Politics* (New York: Basic Books, 1972), and David Shaw, "Political Polls: How to Avoid the Distortions," *Los Angeles Times,* January 3, 1975.

[17] Elmo Roper, "Polls and Sampling," *Saturday Review,* XLIII (October 8, 1960), 58. Italics in original.

[18] *Congressional Record* (February 11, 1960), p. 2,203.

[19]*Ibid.,* p. 2,204. See also Harold Mendelsohn and Irving Crespi, *Polls, Television and the New Politics* (Scranton, Pa.: Chandler, 1970).

[20]"Standards for Reporting Public Opinion Polls," mimeographed release of the American Association for Public Opinion Research (September 27, 1968).

[21] Lucien N. Nedzi, "Public Opinion Polls: Will Legislation Help?" *Public Opinion Quarterly,* XXXV (1971), 340. For hearings on the Nedzi bill, see *Public Opinion Polls: Hearings Before the Subcommittee on Library and Memorials of the Committee on House Administration,* September 19-21 and October 5, 1972 (Washington, D.C.: U.S. Government Printing Office, 1973).

[22] George D. Wolf, "The Scranton Papers" (Paper delivered at the Pennsylvania Historical Association Meeting, October 20, 1967).

[23] For general discussions of polling and campaign management see Dan Nimmo, *The Political Persuaders* (Englewood Cliffs, N.J.: Prentice-Hall, Inc., 1970), and John S. Saloma, *Congress and the New Politics* (Boston: Little, Brown, Inc., 1969).

[24]*New York Times,* October 2, 1972.

[25] See Ithiel Pool *et al., Candidates, Issues, and Strategies: A Computer Simulation of the 1960 and 1964 Presidential Elections* (Cambridge, Mass.: M.I.T. Press, 1965).

[26] Sam Tuchman and Thomas E. Coffin, "The Influence of Election Night Television Broadcasts in a Close Election," *Public Opinion Quarterly,* XXXV (1971), 325-6. See also Kurt Lang and Gladys Engel Lang, *Voting and Nonvoting: Implications of Broadcast Returns Before the Polls are Closed* (Waltham, Mass.: Blaisdell, 1968).

4 Learning Opinions

We know little about the details of either the biophysical or psychological processes of opinion formation and change. We know more, however, about the relations between opinions and the observable elements of personality and behavior. Some of what we know — or what we surmise — about these matters will be reviewed later. Here we may only summarize two points related to the integration of opinions with the individual's total personality, self-image, and effectiveness in small- and large-group situations.

The first point is that opinions must be at least to some degree consistent with observable reality. In large and common matters, an opinion must reflect a reasonably accurate understanding (or at least perception) of objective fact. A person may believe quite honestly that no slums exist in City A; but if on every criterion by which slums are measured it is clear that they *do* exist, this person has been unable to achieve a good "fit" between objective fact and subjective opinion. When such a fit is only mildly incongruous, we put it down, usually, to the person's indifference to fact or to bad judgment; when the fit is notoriously poor, it may mean psychosis.

We must be careful, of course, not to overemphasize the need for opinions to square with fact. It is a matter of everyday observation that prejudice, personal interest, and opinions received uncritically as political (or religious or economic) ideology seem to produce an extraordinary capacity to ignore the most elementary facts.

The second point is that opinions must be, in some general and over-all sense, comfortable to the individual. This consideration is partly a matter of the correspondence the opinions bear to observable and measurable reality — most persons in reasonably good mental health will not be comfortable with opinions that contradict what they see and experience in the world about them. But it is more than mere fit with unambiguous experience, because most opinions on public issues cannot be based on objective fact alone. On public matters facts and experience *are* ambiguous; they are capable of various and often quite contrary interpretations. The opinions of publics cluster around matters about which honest people, honestly viewing the evidence, honestly disagree.

Consequently, except in extreme cases, opinions cannot be judged solely on their congruence with facts; except in extreme cases, where aberrant opinions are accompanied by aberrant behavior, it is hardly a good measure of the worth of an opinion to say that it is not in accord with the facts. Nor is it enough for the opinion holder constantly to test views against the facts. It is important that that be done, of course, and that one be aware of the rationalization processes that so often shape facts to opinions. But no matter how candid one's self-criticism, the test of fit is not sufficient when, as in all large public controversies, the nature of reality is so imperfectly known.

It is therefore, in a sense, as proper as it is inevitable that what we believe and hold as public opinion is to some degree shaped by our personality needs and our self-image. Within the range of opinions that may adequately fit the facts — or on matters in which judgment, insight, creativity, and other individual traits are the decisive opinion producers — each individual selects the view that best suits personal needs.

THE RELATION OF INDIVIDUAL OPINION-HOLDING TO PUBLIC OPINION AND POLITICAL BEHAVIOR

Why is it important to concern ourselves, in a book on *public* opinion, with the psychology of individual opinion holding? For instance, why has it been useful to consider both the neuropsychological equipment with which the individual forms and modifies opinions *and* the personality factors that appear to be related (perhaps in some casual way) to the kinds of views the individual finds comfortable?

As I see it, the importance is not merely the obvious fact that publics consist of individuals, and that the views of publics are therefore the collected views of individuals. This fact is important, to be sure, and if we are to avoid the mysticism of the "great being" view of the public, we must bear it in mind.

Beyond that, the study of personality characteristics of political leaders is even more important. Personality quirks of leaders can have political consequences far beyond their clinical significance. There are, of course, the celebrated cases of the madness of George III and Ivan the Terrible, and the reputed madness of Adolf Hitler. There are the much criticized but still intriguing works of George and George on Woodrow Wilson and Erikson on Martin Luther[1]; such cases illustrate the significance of psychological factors on elite opinion and on public policy.

At a lower but still elite level, that of the political activist, it is likewise important to have an understanding of the psychodynamics of opinion forming. For the political strategist (and the student of political strategy), it is also important to know why some opinions more than others appeal to individuals. Much of the concern with political "images" seems to center on the appeals certain candidates have to ordinary voters. These appeals seem to be related, at least in part, to ideal types that voters want candidates to approximate, and to basic personality needs that some candidate-policy combinations seem to satisfy better than other candidate-policy combinations. These matters, like so much else in political life, are far from being understood; but there is ample evidence that the investigation of individual opinion holding can contribute importantly to the social scientist's study of public opinion and political behavior.

DOES BEHAVIOR FOLLOW OPINION?

As is so often the case, one of the simplest questions that can be put to the analyst of public opinion is one of the most difficult: Does behavior follow opinion? Is there any reason to believe that people act consistently with their beliefs? Do people vote the way they think, for example? or the way they would like to? or the way they say they are going to?

The literature of opinion and attitude study almost invariably assumes that, barring lies and views stated under duress, opinion is always consistent with attitude. This is probably an accurate assumption, as far as it goes. But it is subject to the qualification that lies and views stated under duress are quite common occurrences in attitude and opinion measurement. Racially bigoted persons often give verbal responses (recorded as opinions) quite different from the bigoted attitudes they hold. There are other examples of social pressure to conform to widely held norms and ideals; these may be thought of as problems in the measurement of opinion and, since they were earlier alluded to briefly, will not be reviewed here. It is enough to point out that recorded opinions are not, in fact, always consistent with attitudes, although it is conceptually proper and operationally satisfactory, in most cases, to assume that they are.

It is of greater importance to inquire whether attitudes and opinions are *followed* by behavior. Earlier writers seem to have assumed that behavior was consistent with attitude and opinion; but after carefully reviewing the research on the relationship between what people say their attitudes are and what they actually do, Wicker says ". . . caution must be exercised to avoid making the claim that a given study or set of studies of verbal attitudes, however well done, is socially significant. Most socially significant questions involve overt behavior, rather than people's feelings, and the assumption that feelings are directly translated into actions has not been demonstrated."[2]

What does this mean? One explanation is that a set of social and economic pressures acts on respondents answering an impersonal interview or questionnaire, and another, quite different, set of pressures acts on them when they have to engage in real behavior. Whatever the reasons, it is obvious that we do not always act according to our beliefs. It is no doubt true that some limits must exist to the amount of dissimulation the healthy personality can tolerate. We could not always, or even most of the time, behave in ways contrary to our feelings and opinions. We need to feel that, in general, we speak and do as we honestly think and believe. But this basic sense of personality integration and consistency can be achieved, for most people, at the same time that a good deal of conscious and unconscious dissembling goes on. For, in the first place, our attitudes and opinions are not always clear and uncontradictory; conflicting attitudes make room for conflicting behavior. In the second place, there is a wide social tolerance, even expectation, for the use of little lies, acceptable phrases, circumlocutions, and other forms of behavior that are inconsistent with real attitudes and opinions.

It may be argued, too, that political life allows – perhaps even demands – a greater amount of dissembling at every level of involvement than do other arenas of human activity. Whether this is true or not, it is important to bear in mind that, although both common sense and theories of personality point in the direction of a general correspondence between beliefs and behavior, there are many occasions when behavior will not be consistent with attitudes or opinions. The study of public opinion must therefore be paralleled by and compared in every possible way with the study of political behavior.

OPINIONS AND THE POLITICAL CULTURE

The opinions of average citizens of any country will be heavily influenced by the political culture of which they are a part. *Political culture* has been defined as "the ways in which political elites make decisions, their norms and attitudes as well as the norms and attitudes of the ordinary citizen, his relation to government and to his fellow citizens."[3]

Elazar has applied the concept of political culture – in his case, political *subculture* – to civic attitudes and behavior in the United States. He says that the usual American orientations toward politics and government are "rooted in two contrasting attitudes: . . . in the first, the political order is conceived as a marketplace in which the primary public relationships are products of bargaining among individuals and groups acting out of self-interest." Cities, states, or regions in America dominated by that perspective have what Elazar calls an individualistic political subculture. In the other orientation "the political order is conceived to be a commonwealth – a state in which the whole people have an undivided interest – in which the citizens cooperate in an effort to create and maintain the best government in order to implement certain shared moral principles"[4]; this Elazar calls the moralistic political subculture. There is, finally, a third kind of political subculture in America. This is a preindustrial orientation "rooted in an ambivalent attitude toward the marketplace coupled with a paternalistic and elitist conception of the commonwealth."[5] Although the use of the concept is difficult – because it is necessarily complex, protean, and imprecise – it does seem to be helpful for understanding public opinion in America. Most citizens are influenced very heavily by the common traditions and habits and attitudes of their friends and neighbors with regard to government and politics — and the most apolitical citizens seem to have no other sources of influence. These common traditions, habits, and attitudes constitute the political subculture. To understand that is to understand a very great part of political opinion in America.

POLITICAL SOCIALIZATION GENERALLY

"Political socialization" is a concept that has received a good deal of attention in the last twenty years. It is, as the phrase implies, the application of the older notion of socialization to political beliefs, attitudes, and behavior. In its largest sense, socialization refers to the process by which individual human beings learn (and are taught) the ideas and behaviors that enable them to get along with others. It is the learning and teaching of getting along with others in the world. Most of the simple and elementary beliefs, attitudes, and behaviors necessary to collective existence are learned early in life; hence there is a tendency to associate socialization with infancy and childhood. But it should be clear that socialization consists also of marginal attitude and behavior changes and in the filling in of the cognitive maps and affective schemas by which we all live.[6]

Langton defines *political* socialization as ". . . the process, mediated through various agencies of society, by which an individual learns politically relevant attitudinal dispositions and behavior patterns."[7] The *agencies* of socialization "include such environmental categories as the family, peer group, school, adult organizations, and the mass media." The research on political socialization focuses, for examples, on the learning of attitudes and behavior related to political legitimacy, the way governmental decisions are or should be made, feelings of confidence or cynicism toward politics, and proper or improper uses of authority. "Thus the concept of political socialization is as broad in its empirical referents as those aspects of social behavior that can be meaningfully related to politics."

Andrain has summarized the research findings on childhood political socialization in America. The main result of early citizenship training is the development of superficial, somewhat stylized, benign, and nonconflictful images of government and politics. The children of middle America are told, and believe, that government and political decision-making is protective, benevolent, and based on moral values. As children grow older their sources of information become more varied, their understandings become somewhat more complex (though very few teenagers, or adults, become truly sophisticated about politics), their ability in reality-testing is increased, and they become less stereotypically supportive and more cynical. As would be expected, children of deprived and harsher subcultures, urban blacks and Appalachian poor, learn earlier the more adult patterns of political ambivalence and distrust.[8]

INFLUENCE OF THE FAMILY ON OPINIONS

"Blood is thicker than water." "As the twig is bent so grows the tree." "Like father like son." With these and many other sayings, the unknown historians of folk wisdom testify to the importance of the family in the shaping of opinion and behavior. One of the ways in which the rigid cultural patterns of the past bore most heavily on the individual was in the imposition of strict role and status responsibilities on each member of the family. In learning these responsibilities, and the related folklore of the tribe, the children learned to accept the views of their elders as proper and unchallengeable.

Consciously and unconsciously, parents indoctrinate their children. What is good and bad, what is right and wrong, what is naughty and nice, what is proper and improper – by direct command and advice, by indirect references, and by setting examples, parents shape children to their own values and beliefs. This process is an inevitable and necessary part of socialization, of making little humans fit to live in a sort of social close-order drill with other humans little and big. It gives stability to the culture, predictability for day-to-day social relations, and – not least importantly – tranquillity to family life.

Children imitate their parents. Like parental indoctrination, child-hood imitation is both conscious and unconscious. To use the terminology of the sociologist, the ideal role model for the daughter is almost always her mother; for the son, his father. There is some evidence that the influence of the parental model decreases as the child grows older and she finds other models from among her wider social contacts; but the importance of the parent as a person to be imitated almost never wholly disappears, and it is strongest when the child's opinions and personality are the most malleable.

Members of a family are influenced by the same environmental stimuli. This fact is an important cause of the similarity of opinions within the family, although it is apt to be overlooked if we focus too attentively on the interpersonal influence within the family. All the family is influenced by the same neighbors and neighborhood, by the same friends (who usually share with the family such social characteristics as class, religion, and ethnicity), and by the same economic forces of the area and of the father's occupation. The family members read the same newspapers, attend to the same radio and TV programs, listen to the same preachers and other local opinion leaders, gather the same gossip, and hear the same stories. Exposed as they are, day in and day out, to identical, similar, and convergent stimuli, it is no wonder that families exhibit a marked uniformity of opinion.

The view that the family is the principal agent for political socialization has been widely accepted. Yet, a number of investigators have concluded that school, teenage peer groups, and work groups may be of equal or greater importance.

In America the family seems to be especially influential in establishing some basic political values and orientations of the individual. Using data from a 1965 national sample of high school seniors, Langton and Karns report that for developing a sense of political efficacy in teenagers the family is considerably more important than school or peer group.[9] Political party preference, too, seems to depend more strongly on family than on other socialization agencies.

In their study of the 1948 election, Berelson and his colleagues found that, overall, 75 percent of first voters cast their ballots as their fathers did. Perhaps more interesting is the fact that among adults in families living together, and among those who had made up their minds in October, over 90 percent agreed in their voting intentions.[10] This fact is interesting, yes, but it is hardly surprising either that there should be very high agreement among adults of the same generation, or of several generations, when they choose to remain together as a family unit, and that there should be high (but not quite so high) agreement between parents and children for whom the parental ties have become loosened.[11]

Though some basic political orientations seem to be strongly shaped by the family, it does not appear to be more important than other socialization agencies for influencing opinions on issues. Connell has reviewed nearly forty studies of paired parent-child attitudes and opinions on political issues since 1930. He finds that there is persistent agreement between pairs of parents and children, but that the pair correspondence is also weak (median value about .2, and not the .5 correspondence that Hyman reported finding in 12 studies). Connell confirmed that party preference, as mentioned above, is strongly shared by parent-children pairs, but that attitudes and opinions on "war and communism, political involvement, prejudice, achievement values, and family roles" are less commonly shared. Connell's conclusion is worth quoting:

> To sum up: it appears from a substantial body of evidence that processes within the family have been largely irrelevant to the formation of specific opinions. It appears that older and younger generations have developed their opinions in parallel rather than in series, by similar experiences in a common way of life. The only case where family inheritance of specific opinion can be held to be strong is where the family's communications are clearly shaped by institutions outside it. On both counts we are forced back toward sociological explanations of the patterns of mass belief. That children may gain from their parents some idea of the range of acceptable opinions is quite likely. That specific opinions generally come with mother's milk is — for America, 1944-1968 — rather decisively disproved.[12]

Families living together are almost certain to show higher agreement of attitudes and opinion than are families living apart. Note that there is no causal implication here; living apart may be cause or result of, or have no relation to, differences of opinion. The point is merely that, although distance *may* make the heart grow fonder, it is *almost certain* to weaken the influences that produce like opinions among families and strengthen those that produce unlike opinions.

Within families, disagreement of opinion comes primarily from cross pressures that result when stimuli are not shared equally by all members of the family. Perhaps the most important of these pressures are the effects of different levels and types of education within a family. Children *learn* to disagree with their parents; and the disagreements tend to be more profound if this learning involves not just new information but new values and life styles — as when the children of newly arrived immigrants go to Ameircan schools, or the daughter of the Southern hill farmer attends a prestige Eastern college. Like-mindedness within families is weakened by differences in economic stimuli, as when the son "graduates" from his father's haberdashery to the big department store or when he leaves the farm to become a railroad brakeman. Differences in social status seem to be important, as when the daughter of the shoemaker marries the local physician or the newly rich oil driller joins the country club. Finally, changing family roles tend to create opinion differences, as when a daughter becomes a mother and follows the advice of Dr. Spock rather than that of her mother. Each of these clusters of influence — educational, economic, social status, and role — will be considered separately, albeit briefly, below. Here it is enough to say that they interact with — sometimes reinforcing, sometimes weakening — opinion agreement within families.[13]

RELIGION AND SOCIOPOLITICAL ATTITUDES

Organized religion in America interacts with political opinion in two ways. First, it provides much of what might be called "background values" for individual and group behavior. The cultural values of any society are likely to have their roots in sacred traditions or doctrines, even if they have been highly secularized in the way they are presented. Greenstein found that many of the New Haven schoolchildren he talked with confused religious and political symbolism: They saw the national anthem as akin to church music, and they thought of the authority of the United States President as somehow like that of God. And, of course, the divine right of kings was an idea accepted by many adults three hundred years ago.

But one hardly needs to assume a direct association of Godpower with kingpower to appreciate that some general attitudes stressed by religious groups in America may be among the causes of and reinforcements for *political* tendencies and preferences of our citizens. I suggest that there are three basic tendencies of American religious experience that help to provide the "background values" for political behavior. They are (1) Jewish and Catholic self-righteousness, and (2) the "Protestant ethic," and (3) religious fundamentalism. A comment on each:

Jewish and Catholic Self-Righteousness

I refer by this phrase to the central doctrine of exclusivity that has informed both Judaism and Catholicism during much of their histories. It says, oversimplified: "We are superior to peoples who have other religious beliefs, and we feel obliged to show our superiority by (1) criticizing their beliefs, (2) boycotting their presence, or (3) converting them to our way." There is some irony in the historic fact that the early Christians rejected the exclusivity of the Jews — although that irony was no doubt little appreciated by the "heretics" of sixteenth-century Spain, or by the "heathens" of seventeenth-century Central America, whose deviations were corrected by the stake or by being confined for their lives to the walls of the mission.

To be the chosen people is a heavy burden indeed. For members of a group to believe that their doctrines and rituals have some special godly sanction is unquestionably an effective basis for solidarity. But the in-group cohesion thus gained is paid for in out-group conflict and hatred. And the point here is that religious self-righteousness provides a way of thinking that affects everyday political opinions and actions. The Jewish prohibitions against intermarriage with persons of other faiths; the Catholic dictum, held until very recently, that the Jews collectively were responsible for the death of Christ; or the doctrine of "vincible ignorance," suggesting that certain non-Catholics are eternally damned — these are religious supports for American "background values" that are still strong. The story (perhaps apocryphal) about a papal legate during one of the "heresy wars" illustrates the kind of thinking encouraged by "chosen people" doctrines. A field commander came to him, it is said, with the dilemma, "The heretics and believers look the same. How can we tell them apart?" To which the legate replied: "Kill them all. God will know his own." Respect for the individual is easily lost in the clash of self-righteous groups.

The Protestant Ethic

The concept of the Protestant ethic refers not merely to an attitude toward work or to a personal code of strait-laced morality, though both those views are often used as though they were synonymous with the concept. It seems generally more accurate to say that the Protestant ethic is a concentration of attitudinal emphases that, individually, may be thought of as a subculture. Here the concept is dealt with only in its social sense, as a subculture.[14]

The historic ties between Protestantism and capitalism have been described by Weber and Tawney.[15] Their claims that those two great social movements were related ideologically and attitudinally seem to me quite persuasive. Their evidence and arguments cannot be repeated here, even in summary fashion; it may only be noted that, historically, many theories and opinions of the early modern period — the importance of freedom of choice for individuals, the philosophy of salvation through work, the religious and economic colonization of newly discovered land, and the breakdown of restrictions regarding money and credit — hastened and reinforced the growth of capitalism and Protestantism alike.

Two caveats are in order. First, the Weber-Tawney argument is historical, reflecting Protestantism from the sixteenth century to World War I; it says little explicitly about Protestantism of the late twentieth century. Second, capitalism was initially a form of economic radicalism; and, although it is no longer radical in the West, it can hardly be described as having been a conservative doctrine during most of the period about which Weber and Tawney wrote.

A powerful "background value" in American society is that of *independence* — which seems to mean the ability to make one's way economically and to be free of burdensome social restraints. Americans do not want others either to give them charity or to give them personal advice. Despite the rhetoric of conservative groups in America (and the occasional laments of high federal officials that there is a turning away from self-reliance), people on welfare are as committed to the work ethic as middle-class people.[16] An underlying impulse to self-sufficiency was found by Robert Lane in his depth interviews with fifteen working-class men in New Haven. Although they were not very knowledgeable about political issues or about the candidates they voted for, they made little effort to get additional information or help in making up their minds. They appeared to believe that individual citizens could somehow sense, by intuition or some unnamed human virtue, what was right and proper in political matters. Lane calls this stubborn and irrational individualism a belief in "the parthenogenesis (that is, the virgin birth) of knowledge."[17] I think it is not too far-fetched to relate such tenacious, if naive, political individualism to the Protestant ethic. Just as Protestantism itself means, at bottom, the rejection of the authority of religious specialists and experts in favor of the view that each Christian has to get a personal truth out of the sacred word, so it gives strength to a powerful "background value" of self-sufficiency in political attitudes and opinions.

Further, one finds in the lives of American political leaders evidence of the Protestant ethic. President Wilson's biographers are agreed that a stern morality of individual accountability and social reform motivated him so strongly that it damaged his political effectiveness.[18] And Milton Viorst says about former Secretary of State Dean Rusk:

> [He] readily acknowledges the influence that his father's Protestant religion had on him. He has said that when he was young, most of his home life was built around the church. He was faithful in his attendance at Sunday school and midweek prayer meetings. . . . it is impossible to understand [Rusk] without grasping the meaning of Southern Protestantism . . . . Basic to it is a rigid Calvinism, with the commitment to Original Sin and the essential evil of most men, with the obverse that the Saved will eschew frivolity and lead lives of abnegation and sacrifice.[19]

Fundamentalism

Related to the Protestant ethic, yet different, is the third religiously based quality that appears to shape the "background values" of many Americans. Wolfinger and his collaborators investigated the political attitudes and motivations of several hundred participants in a "Christian Anti-Communism Crusade" in 1962. They found that on most personality and socioeconomic measurements the Christian Crusaders did not differ much from other American adults. They were, in fact, rather better informed than most Americans on public issues, and did not seem to be especially authoritarian in their general thinking. What they shared in unusual degree was a quality the researchers labeled as fundamentalism. They listed the following elements of "fundamentalist beliefs and intellectual style which are compatible with radical right interpretations of history":

1. Belief in the literalness and purity of Biblical teachings makes fundamentalists resistant to change.
2. They are affronted by moral relativism, increasingly lenient sexual mores, the decline of parental authority, and other aspects of the secular modern world.
3. The fundamentalist sees "the world as strictly divided into the saved and the damned, the forces of good and the forces of evil."

4. The main danger to the faithful is from the corrosion of faith
   by invidious doctrines — a danger from within.[20]

In addition to the creation of sociopolitical "background values,"
religious organizations seem to become more conservative, with regard to
their economic, social, and welfare doctrines, as they become more "successful." Success means membership and material wealth, and the fact
is that radical groups, almost by definition — except in revolutionary
circumstances — have little of either. There is a natural history of successful protest movements — and all religious groups have their beginnings
in protest — that is one of change from small, militant membership out
of step with their time to large, more or less apathetic membership
accepting, and accepted by, the dominant social forces of their time.

It probably cannot be said that the acquisition of wealth alone is
an important factor in the conservatism of church groups. That argument is sometimes made — indeed, it will be made in this book — to
explain in part the political opinions of persons associated with big business. But wealth by itself is not an important factor in producing conservatism in church doctrine and among church leadership. There are at
least three reasons for this: (a) the doctrine of clerical poverty is widely
enough held, even among Protestant sects, that individual wealth among
church leaders offers no temptation to find reason and fairness in the
economic status quo; (b) the wealth of church groups tends to be used
for reformist ends — charity, teaching, and conversion — that daily remind
these groups not only of their own limited resources but of the almost
unlimited need for reform; and, finally (c), one practical result of church
immunity from taxation is that church resources are not reduced, as are
those of wealthy individuals and corporations, by expensive government
welfare policies.

Although it seems unlikely that wealth alone makes churches conservative, size of membership, by itself, may have an important relationship
to the organization's social and political opinion structure. It is doubt-
lessly not just chance that the smallest doctrinally identifiable churches
in America (to distinguish them from personality-centered, local, or
fundamentalist splinter groups) are also the least tolerant of the sociopolitical status quo. The Quakers, Unitarians, Brethren, and Jehovah's
Witnesses are all (though in different ways) quite critical of mass social
and political values in modern life; they remain small in numbers. Roman
Catholics and the larger Protestant denominations seem to be on much

better terms with those values. This fact is not a surprising point, however, since an organization that is generally supportive of the dominant and majority values of a society will by definition be supportive of the status quo, and will therefore gain many adherents, as long as access is not restricted and personal needs are met by membership. Conformity, in such cases, feeds on conformity, and the status quo is unchallenged.

SURVEY RESEARCH ON
RELIGION AND POLITICAL ATTITUDES

The evidence for the claim that church influence in mid-twentieth-century America is predominantly conservative does not come alone from the analysis of doctrine and the official pronouncements of church leadership or policy. Attitude and opinion studies, on the whole, bear out the conservative image of churches and churchgoing. In the three-way breakdown of Protestants, Catholics, and Jews, only Jews are consistently found to express liberal opinions on social and political questions.

Stouffer and his collaborators analyzed data gathered from 4,939 persons in a nationwide probability sample and from 1,533 community leaders in 123 cities in randomly selected sampling areas. Stouffer was concerned with measuring public toleration for political nonconformity in the context of the real and perceived internal and external Communist threat of 1954. He reported that churchgoers are more intolerant of political nonconformity than are nonchurchgoers, in the national sample, whether the results are controlled for sex (that is, when the factors of greater churchgoing by women and greater intolerance by women are taken into account), for education, for age, for degree of interest in issues, or for differences in the perceived dangers of internal Communist threat.[21] There is some inferential evidence from responses in the South that Protestants in that region may be less tolerant of political nonconformity than are Catholics; but this is not to be inferred about the North. Stouffer concludes that

> Regular church attenders are less likely than other people to be tolerant of the kinds of nonconformists or suspected nonconformists about whom we are inquiring. . . .
> There would appear to be something about people who go to

church regularly that makes fewer of them, as compared with non-churchgoers, willing to accord civil rights to nonconformists who might be Communists, suspected Communists, or merely Socialists.[22]

A large sample (4,745) of American Lutherans was interviewed in early 1970; over 700 items were on the questionnaire, but few tapped political attitudes directly. The sample was said to be representative of American Lutheranism: 98 percent white, 96 percent native-born, they were predominantly Scandinavian or German in background, attended church more than the average American Protestant, were above average in formal education, slightly above average in income, average in occupational status, less mobile than the average American, and concentrated in the Midwest.

Political attitudes of American Lutherans seem to be consistent with their base values: a transcendent meaning in life (salvation, forgiveness, a caring God, belief in eternal life), desire for a stable, dependable world, and desire for a controllable world. "Events, programs, ministry, and persons are going to be ranked by most Lutherans in terms of support or threat to these values."[23]

Lutherans express a considerable commitment to liberalism and to a just society: 80 percent think the elimination of all racial discrimination is a goal of Christianity; 87 percent would regard alcoholics and drug addicts as disease victims rather than criminals; and 68 percent say "every person has a right to adequate housing, even if he cannot afford it." On the other hand, 69 percent of the Lutherans interviewed objected to blacks and whites dating; 19 percent would not want alcoholics and 38 percent would not want drug addicts in their community; and 77 percent agreed that "poor people would be better off if they took advantage of the opportunities available to them rather than spending so much time protesting." Sixty percent were in favor of the death penalty in 1970.

The picture of the Lutheran faithful that emerges is one of socially conforming, law-abiding, change-resistant, and on the whole nonparticipating citizens. On the Bogardus "social distance scales" they turn out to be apprehensive of persons and groups whose life styles are perceived as different: hippies, homosexuals, drug addicts, alcoholics, and atheists. Among generally unacceptable groups to Lutherans in 1970 were three that were perceived as political: Communists lead the list for unacceptability; Students for a Democratic Society are more acceptable than homosexuals, drug addicts, and hippies; John Birch Society members are, in turn, more acceptable than alcoholics and atheists. Few Lutherans have *ever* personally contacted a public official on a controversial issue (14 percent), publicly taken a stand on an issue (11 percent), publicly supported a political candidate (12 percent), or circulated a petition (9 percent); they are about equally divided on the abstract principle of whether their church doctrines "encourage active participation in social reform" (48 percent agree, 43 percent disagree).

The Jews are the only religious group that, in every study and measurement, are more liberal than the American norm. Stouffer classified 79 percent of the Jewish males (N = 76) and 68 percent of the Jewish females (N = 82) as "more tolerant" on his scale, as compared with 31 percent of the whole national sample so classified.[24] In October 1954, the Survey Research Center obtained information about political attitudes and voting patterns of Protestants, Catholics, and Jews. There were no important differences between the Protestant and Catholic responses on United States involvement in world affairs or on the need for more domestic social legislation, but the Jewish respondents were significantly more internationalist and supportive of social legislation.[25]

After examining earlier work, and on the basis of his own survey in Jewish wards in Boston, Fuchs declared:

> The results of all of these studies show American Jews to be economic liberals — twentieth-century style — almost without regard to differences in class lines within the group, and despite the fact that Jews as a group are now perched near if not on the top of the economic class ladder.
>
> In foreign policy matters, the Jews have been internationalists.[26]

There has been much speculation about the sources of Jewish social and political liberalism. Many commentators have seen it as a result of centuries of Jewish minority-consciousness and of their oppression by non-Jewish majorities. Historic underdogs themselves, they tend to take the side of the underdog who needs collective help in material ways (social welfare) and who welcomes political and other kinds of change. Analyzing Jewish social attitudes as they relate to political opinions and behavior, Fuchs suggests that a cluster of more or less characteristically Jewish values underlie Jewish liberalism. "What are the distinctive values of America's Jewish subculture?" he asks.

To judge from a vast impressionistic literature and a growing systematic study of Jewish culture, those things most valued by Jews as Jews are: (1) Learning (Torah); (2) Charity (Zedakeh); and, for want of a better phrase or word, (3) Life's pleasures (nonasceticism). In probably no other American subculture is so high a value placed upon learning and intellectuality, or upon the helping of the poor by the rich and the weak by the strong, or upon living a good life upon earth in full use of one's body. These three values, taken together or regarded separately, have helped to guide Jewish political behavior in recent decades along what in the discourse of our times would be called "liberal lines."[27]

Religion and Political Action. With regard to partisan affiliation the religious pattern in America has been reasonably clear since the 1930s. Protestants tend to be Republicans,[28] Catholics tend to be Democrats, and Jews are overwhelmingly Democrats. There is a positive association between strength of attachment to religion and strength of attachment to party; that is, Catholics closely identified with their religion vote more Democratic than Catholics not so closely identified with their church, and closely identified Protestants vote more Republican. Conversely, those who are more closely identified with *politics* are influenced less by their religious persuasions. One study found that in the event of political cross-pressure between religion and social class, young voters are more apt to resolve the conflicts in favor of class.[29]

It may be that the relationships between religion and partisanship are gradually washing out in America. The Berelson study, as noted, suggested that economic and social-class influences are generally more important than religious influences for young men and women. There is scattered impressionistic evidence that the propensity for Catholics to be Democrats is not so strong as it has been historically in America. The 1960 election between Protestant Republican Richard Nixon and Catholic Democrat John Kennedy was the occasion for a temporary display, and even exaggeration, of the older feeling that the Democrats were the party of "Romanism" and the Republicans were Protestant-controlled. It is unclear just how important religious attitudes and affiliations were for voter choice in 1960. There was undeniably a drift of Republican Catholics to Kennedy and a drift of Democratic Protestants to Nixon. But it seems also undeniable that for most people, the *party* loyalties were stronger than religious counterpressures. A considerable amount of what appeared to be religiously based switching was probably either Catholics coming back to their regular base in the Democratic party after flirting with Eisenhower Republicanism in the 1950s or Southern

Protestants, historically Democratic, who were moving to the G.O.P. for reasons that had nothing to do with religion.[30] There is also some merit in the suggestion that, with the election of a Catholic president in 1960, the importance of religious preferences and biases has declined as an influence on aggregate voting behavior.[31]

While there may be an erosion of Catholic support for the Democratic Party and its candidates, it does not appear, at least as yet, to be a major fact of American political demography. Table 4.1 indicates that Catholics may be less strongly supportive of the Democratic Party, and more "independent" in their self-designations. "There have been changes in how Catholic voters identify with the two major parties, but none of the sort that presage a generation of Republicanism."[32]

TABLE 4-1.   Catholic Voters' Party Identification, 1967 and 1972

	Strong Democrat	Mainly Democrat	Independent	Mainly Republican	Strong Republican
1967	25%	27%	28%	10%	5%
1972	17%	30%	35%	11%	5%

Source: Mark R. Levy and Michael S. Kramer, *The Ethnic Factor.* Copyright © 1972, 1973, by the Institute of American Research, Inc. Reprinted by permission of Simon and Schuster.

In general, and almost always on matters thought of traditionally as "political" (e.g., elections, appointments, and party organization), clergy and parishioners alike seem to think that there ought to be a fairly clear separation of church and politics. In a study of the opinions of more than fifteen hundred Episcopalians, Ringer and Glock relate that "few parishioners expect the church to stay out of politics altogether"; most think the minister should urge his church members to study the issues and to vote, but only one-fourth would allow candidates to speak in the church buildings, and fewer than one in ten would approve their minister's endorsing a candidate. In short, "the more the minister's activity would thrust him into the political arena as an active participant, the more hesitant are parishioners to voice approval."[33]

The Lutheran study suggests that Protestants may be more willing to support activist ministers in 1970 than they were in 1952. Among 1970 respondents 67 percent would approve clergymen's taking stands (not in the pulpit) on public issues, and 56 percent would approve support of a political candidate (not in the pulpit). Twenty five percent would approve a pulpit sermon on a political issue. However, there are limits to parishioners' support for an activist clergy: 21 percent approved clergymen's participation in civil rights protest marchers (76 percent disapproved); 17 percent approved their participation in antiwar protest marches, and 10 percent would support their clergy in civil disobedience that risked arrest (38 percent "disapproved" and 48 percent "strongly disapproved").[34]

EDUCATION AND OPINION-HOLDING

Although the influence of formal education is much investigated, little is known about the ways in which schools create or re-create opinion. However — as is often the case in the analysis of opinion correlates — though we fail to trace the labyrinth of detail, some large patterns of influence may be observed.

After the family, the school is perhaps the most powerful institution of the society in its impact on what is thought by whom on what issues. The average school cannot re-form the opinion network of the average child; this is too certainly determined by the family and its environment. But the extraordinary school (there are a few) and the extraordinary teacher (there are many, though never enough) can sometimes re-form the opinions of the average child. What is more important, such schools and teachers (and, sometimes, even ordinary schools and teachers) can shape the opinions and often the whole life of the above-average child.

In the schools, whether public or private, the creation of opinion leaders begins. This is a sociopolitical function of the schools that, so far as I know, has been little remarked — perhaps because it is as obvious as it is significant. In the public schools the child for the first time is systematically exposed to as great a variety of people and opinion as the school district affords. The narrow world of family, playmates, and parents' church is supplemented by a routinized but deliberately innovative social institution that not only tolerates but increasingly encourages opinion variety. One of the distinguishing and most significant characteristics of the American public school is that it is the first occasion for the nonvoluntary exposure of the individual to persons with whom she may have little in common except membership in a political community. This exposure constitutes the first direct impact of the polity on the individual. Until she enters the public school, she contacts the public (through government) only indirectly; but on her first day of class, and thereafter for ten, twelve, sixteen, or twenty years, she is obliged to follow some rules, to take note of some differences (and similarities), and to engage actively or passively in social controversies big and little. Parents start the socialization process, but at least one importance of the public schools is that, by virtue of the greatly expanded sociopolitical exposure, the socialization process is enlarged by a quantum leap.

Now, it should not be thought, just because the scope of community influence on the child is significantly expanded upon entering the public school, that this influence will radically alter or conflict with the values and habits that family and preschool environment have endowed. The schools may in some ways conflict with home conditioning, but the conflicts are usually not many or starkly presented. The hand of the state is on the child for the first time; but it is the gentle hand of a local school board and of local teachers, who are least aware of their political nature — and who, since they define politics in the traditional but narrow sense of party antagonisms, in fact deny their political nature (which is, perhaps, just as well). The major thrust of the schools is thus, at least in the early years, the reinforcement of family attitudes and family opinions; for although the social heterogeneity of the child's environment is significantly expanded, she is shielded from the full effect of this heterogeneity by a curriculum that attends mainly to common fact-gathering and superficial (if, at this stage, important) social graces.

The schools in any society are necessarily one of the major institutions for the conservation of traditional values. One American social anthropologist argues that a public school system cannot, by its very nature, act as a change-producing force. "American classrooms," he says, "like educational institutions anywhere, express the values, preoccupations, and fears found in the culture as a whole. School has no choice; it must train the children to fit the culture as it is. School can give training in skills; it cannot teach creativity."[35]

I think that view is too simple and too pessimistic. There is, of course, a genuine question whether any person or any institution can *teach* creativity. But some conditions are more favorable to creativity than others, and schools and teachers may — even if they seldom do — provide in part those favorable conditions. The old ways, "the culture as it is," may be challenged daily in American classrooms, even though the overarching purpose of an educational system is admittedly (and necessarily) the shaping of young minds and behavior to acceptable and traditional ways.

The significance of school textbooks for reflecting dominant cultural values, and changes in these over time, was measured by DeCharms and Moeller. Themes representing economic and technological achievement increased in number from 1800 to 1900, then decreased to 1950. Themes representing interpersonal affiliation (an index of David Riesman's "other-directed" orientation) generally increased over the 150-year period. And what the authors call "moral teaching" was drastically reduced from high to almost zero over the century and a half.[36]

Merriam noted that conditions peculiar to the United States make it likely that the United States school system will be a more influential opinion-forming institution than the European school system: (a) the influence of the home is weakened by the migratory character of our people and (b) the influence of religion by the variety of competing systems of religion, which weakens the force of any one of them. Because of these conditions, it might be assumed that the influence of the school in America would be *pro tanto* greater than that of the school in Europe, and, to some extent, this is true.[37] These characteristics of American society, with their probable effect on the importance of the schools as value-forming institutions, are as significant in the 1970s as they were when noted by Merriam more than thirty years ago.

I wish to emphasize, however, that I am talking about the general values and the basic attitudes that the school and the community share in considerable degree. Though the process at the beginning, and in the early grades, is one of learning and reinforcing the simplest and most fundamental skills, what is learned as the level of schooling goes up increasingly becomes a filling in of the meanings of values, the relations of these values to the "real" world, and a greater specificity of attitudes and attitude constellations — along with a greater storehouse of fact and evidential material related (often in very simple ways) to value and attitude. Generally, what we hold in our minds of ideas, things, and persons changes through the educational process and institutions from fuzzy to less fuzzy. Like the infant's early learning of shapes and colors, the later educational process is one of increasingly subtle differentiation; things and ideas become more clearly distinguished from other things and ideas. Accompanying this differentiation is the increasingly more subtle ability to reintegrate things and ideas in ways that have wider meaning.

FORMAL POLITICAL
SOCIALIZATION IN THE SCHOOLS

Social and political indoctrination, conscious and unconscious, clearly exists in public schools. Some such indoctrination in the values of a democratic society is necessary — for "fair play" in school becomes due process in law, and "citizenship" becomes protection of minority rights. Other kinds of values no doubt impede the search for truth that educators everywhere profess to be their goal.

How much of this indoctrination "takes," and how does the school compare in importance with other agents of political socialization? Hyman and some others believe the family to be the most important. Langton says parents and other adults are more influential than age-mates.[38] Hess and Torney suggest that for children of five to thirteen the schools as a whole (teachers, administrators, and fellow students) have more influence than the family for political socialization.[39] Sigelman and Hantke asked Texas high school seniors and university students to differentiate the importance of seven socialization agents with regard to three kinds of values/attitudes. Their findings suggest that it is unfruitful to debate whether home or school or peers are most important — it seems to depend on the question "Important when, and for what?"

> There is a good deal of *topic specialization* among socialization agents. . . . Home and church, traditional social institutions, have their greatest impact on basic values, especially on honesty, and have less influence on political opinions. The media, on the other hand, are particularly influential with respect to political opinions, and markedly less so for social attitudes and basic values. Topic specialization is less obvious for the two remaining agents, though schools do appear to have less impact on social attitudes than on basic values or political opinions.[40]

Experimental studies of indoctrination in the schools bear out the common-sense view that pupils can be influenced by one-sided arguments. As early as 1938 Remmers summarized several experiments on the amount and permanence of induced opinion change. On deliberate attempts to change social and political attitudes, he declared:

> . . . a high school teacher is likely to obtain the kinds of attitudes which are consciously set up as educational objectives and striven for as such. And it appears that unless some specific effort is made to change attitudes they are not likely to change.

Remmers' investigations were followed about a decade later by a comprehensive series of experiments at Yale. In general, the Yale studies corroborated the findings of the earlier work. Other things being equal, exposure is followed immediately by considerable change in the direction indicated by the content of the message; over a short period of time, much of the effect of a single exposure wears off; but there remains a net and lasting (in the absence of countering information) change in the expected direction.[41]

Efforts of schools to change attitudes are more likely to succeed than are experimental efforts to change attitudes. Experiments almost always employ one-shot exposures; schools, on the other hand, again and again, under varied conditions over time, are able to bring to students systematic and reinforcing exposures. The evidence is that repeated, confirmatory, and ego-satisfying stimuli can be produced by the schools. Many of the values so inculcated and reinforced will be the modal values of the community in which the school is located. But many will be wider, "cosmopolitan" rather than "local" values, and will suggest or facilitate conflict and social change.

The paradox is this: Almost all investigators of formal political socialization efforts in American schools believe that those efforts have considerable impact. Yet attempts to measure that impact often show that it is small, or even negligible.

Jaros points out that, on the question of inculcation of political values, the schools could have impact in any one or all of the following ways: "(1) curricular content alone, (2) curricular content mediated by educational quality, (3) teachers' overt expression of their own values in classroom situations, (4) teachers' more casual expression of their own values in less structured, out-of-class situations, and (5) pupil identification with particular teachers and adoption of values these teachers are perceived to hold."[42]

One supposes that schooling could influence young Americans by: (1) shaping their *beliefs, values, and attitudes,* (2) increasing their *knowledge* about government and politics, and (3) motivating or providing opportunities for political *action.* A brief review of the evidence so far indicates the following.

The main impact of schools on beliefs and values seems to be a strengthening and clarifying of political identity (who one is: American, Georgian, Atlantan) and an attachment to vague notions of constitutionalism, First Amendment rights, and partisanship. Hyman and some of the earlier researchers implied that schools taught blind patriotism based on primordial and sacred ties. Easton and Hess report that the "truly formative years of the maturing member of a political system would seem to be the years between the ages of three and thirteen . . . . By the time children have reached second grade (age 7) most of them have become firmly attached to their political community . . . . they have learned that they are Americans . . . . Not only do many children associate the sanctity and awe of religion with the political community, but to ages 9 or 10 they sometimes have considerable difficulty in disentangling God and country."[43] Singing patriotic songs, pledging the flag, prayers in school (even after outlawed), and the offhand, probably unconscious comments of patriotic teachers contribute day in and day out to the perpetuation of narrow patriotism in the public schools. In many middle-sized and smaller communities local patriotic organizations like the American Legion and the DAR have special reinforcing activities in the schools — essay and speech contests with themes like "Why I Am Proud to Be an American," with prizes on Commencement and Class Days. It is easy to see why and how patriotic and nationalistic attitudes are encouraged and fostered in American schools.

There is, however, another and contradictory set of values and attitudes fostered in the schools. These are the values of diversity, toleration, fair play, majority-rule-and-minority-rights. And it is important to note that these are the values that are increasingly called forth over the years of formal schooling (1) as the children become more independent psychologically and socially, (2) as they gather more knowledge about politics and the bases and structures of authority, and (3) as they experience conflict, both generally and in its political forms. These are the civil values. Andrain's responses from fifth- and eighth-grade students in Southern California indicated that civil values, more than sacred or primordial values, provide the basis for patriotism and national identity.[44]

American children and youth quite clearly increase their political *knowledge* as a result of school activity. They learn facts of history and of contemporary events and processes; they also learn the opinions of others, and to some extent they learn how to learn about political things. Andrain's respondents confirm the expectation that eighth-graders know much more than fifth-graders about what he calls "the *content* of political knowledge," thus showing "the effects of increased education and cognitive maturity."[45] As one would also expect, knowledge depends on I.Q. and political interest, but even when these variables are held constant, knowledge increases with increase in schooling. Other investigations at the high school level indicate that civics courses do not significantly increase political knowledge for middle-class students, perhaps because those courses are repetitious and uninformative, but they seem to produce increased knowledge in disadvantaged youngsters, for whom the factual content is new.[46] In short, it is clear that the schools do teach students some historic and current facts about politics, political institutions, and political issues.

What is the evidence on the third possible way the schools might have a political influence on young Americans: Do they provide motivations and opportunities for political activity?

The short answer seems to be that most schools do not provide much incentive, and few provide real opportunity, for political participation. Litt's imaginative and often cited study of three Boston-area schools is instructive: The values and factual content of the civics courses in the two lower-class schools were overwhelmingly those appropriate to "subject" and nonparticipatory citizenship roles; only in the upper-class area was there school content that explored controversy in a realistic way and suggested that citizenship included involvement in the political management of conflict.[47]

Merelman's interviews with sixth-, ninth-, and twelfth-graders, and with their teachers, in two Los Angeles area school districts revealed that interest in participating in politics decreases sharply as students grow older. Among sixth-graders 31 percent said they "would like someday to run for political office"; 18 percent of ninth-graders and only 11 percent of twelfth-graders said they would like to run for office. On this question responses in the wealthier district were the same as in the poorer district. Merelman concludes that: "One recurrent aspect of maturation is sloughing off childhood fantasies about recognition and power. The progressive disparagement of political ambitions may simply be a political expression of this general process . . . . In addition, Americans' ambivalence toward politicians may be so deeply rooted in culture and society as to engulf counterpressures from the schools. Thus it appears that individual growth and cultural sanctions combine to defeat the schools."[48]

There is some evidence that schools increase students' sense of political efficacy — and this, if true, is important for participation, since people who feel they can have influence will, of course, participate more in politics. Among high school seniors in 1965 the schools seem to have been less important than the family, but more important than peer groups, for the development of political efficacy.[49]

No doubt many public high school teachers and administrators minimize participatory values and facts about controversy for fear of criticism from local status quo interests. Such inhibitions are reduced, however, in political socialization at the college level. Yet the generalizations about values, content, and action that are drawn from investigations of junior high and high school students seem rather consistently true at the college level as well. With regard to political action, specifically, the best summary seems to be that

> . . . exposure to courses with political content of various types appears to produce no increment in participatory tendencies . . . . Indeed, one might argue the counter proposition, that knowledge of the political process is just as likely to make students more cynical . . . . In any event, there is apparently nothing inherently productive of conventional democratic participation in the receipt of politically oriented college instruction in the United States today.[50]

FORMAL EDUCATION AND POLITICAL OPINION-HOLDING AMONG AMERICAN ADULTS

The last section summarized what we know about schools as agents of political socialization in America. This section deals with the relationship between formal education and the quantity and quality of political opinion-holding in the American electorate.

Education helps a person to think. The more a person knows, the more he is able to free himself from the restricting viewpoints of his own self and his own experiences. This is perhaps the cardinal sense in which, as the cliche goes, education makes broader horizons. The individual who knows a good deal about other persons, places, and ideas is able more effectively to relate his own existence to his social and physical environment. Opinion surveys reveal, almost without exception, that college graduates have more opinions on more issues than do high school graduates, and high school graduates have more opinions than do grade school graduates. For example, Matthews and Prothro found that among their Southern respondents, both white and black, education was almost perfectly related to a political information test. That relationship is shown in Figure 4-1.

The better-educated have more opinions. The "don't know" responses of poll questions almost invariably confirm this unsurprising fact, that people with more formal education have more opinions on more issues (see Table 4-2).

FIGURE 4-1.   Education and Political Information in the South, by Race

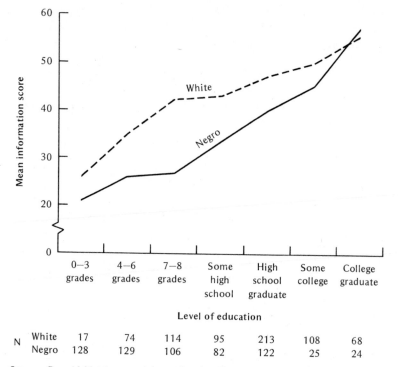

| | White | 17 | 74 | 114 | 95 | 213 | 108 | 68 |
| N | Negro | 128 | 129 | 106 | 82 | 122 | 25 | 24 |

Source: Donald Matthews and James Prothro, *Negroes and the New Southern Politics* (New York: Harcourt Brace Jovanovich, Inc., 1966), p. 79.

Analysis suggests that those with less education may be unwilling or unable to express opinions on foreign issues or complex questions of domestic policy, but that they are as capable as those with more education of answering questions about economic or social policy that affects them as individuals.

A number of analysts have suggested that every person's political behavior is heavily influenced by the confidence she has in the political system of which she is a part. The authors of *The Voter Decides* report that, "as was expected, education is highly related to the efficacy scale; one-half of those respondents who attended college rank high on this scale, as compared with only 15 percent of those who have completed no more than grade school."[51] Later, in *The American Voter*, Campbell and his collaborators point out that this sense of political efficacy is in part a function of income and high-status occupation; but, they declare,

TABLE 4-2. Formal Education and Numbers of "No Opinion" Responses on Selected Issues

	% of No Opinion		
	College	High School	Grade School
"In view of developments since we entered, did U.S. make a mistake in sending troops to Vietnam?" (Feb. 1973)	5	12	16
"Should sellers of hard drugs such as heroin be given life without chance of parole?" (Feb. 1973)	5	4	7
"Are the federal taxes you pay now too high, too low, or about right?" (Mar. 1973)	5	5	10
"Should young men who left the country to avoid the draft be allowed to return without punishment?" (Mar. 1973)	1	3	8
"Should wage-price controls be more strict, less strict, or as they are now?" (May 1973)	7	7	13
"Do you approve American planes' bombing in Cambodia and Laos?" (May 1973)	6	15	22
"With regard to the Watergate affair, has the mass media provided too much coverage, too little, or about the right amount?" (June 1973)	2	6	17

Source: *Gallup Opinion Index*, month indicated.

the fact that it is "more strongly related to education than to other dimensions of status that may symbolize equal strength in the power structure suggests that education contributes to the attitude in a more direct way."[52]

The generalization that the highly educated show more confidence in the political system is supported even more strongly by a study of 779 Oregon adults in 1959. On a six-point Guttman-type scale of "political cynicism," it was found that "the highly educated are much more politically trusting than the least educated. . . . The politically trusting outnumber the political cynics by five to one among the highly educated, while the ratio is 1:1 among the least educated."[53] When the results were controlled for income and occupation, the educational factor was still overwhelmingly important; the "data show clearly that within every income level, the higher the level of education, the lower the proportion of political cynics. The relationship here is both strong and consistent."[54] The highly educated were also found, in this study, to possess a greater sense of "political potency,"[55] which corroborated the findings of earlier studies on this dimension of political confidence.

The effects of educational levels on opinion holding are deftly summarized by Smith in his study of views on world affairs between 1946 and 1956. After reviewing the literature and presenting his own data from AIPO polls, Smith suggested three types of patterns with regard to opinion quantity, stability, and confidence:

Composed of the executive and professional and college groupings, the first international public enjoys an impressive degree of opinion homogeneity on a variety of issues. It exhibits a consistently high level of information and concern about world affairs, reacts quickly and appropriately to events, and evidences more opinion stability than do other publics. . . . While any label will be imperfect, all things considered, the term "engaged public" seems more apt, for it adds the connotation of an active effort to keep informed and to influence policy, an important distinguishing feature of this public. . . .

Smith's middle "international public,"

. . . comprising the white-collar, high-school-educated, and sometimes skilled-worker groupings, exhibits a poorly defined membership-opinion profile. Both the white-collar and skilled-worker segments show distinctive attitude sets of their own, plus puzzling internal inconsistencies; the former often joining the engaged public while the latter erratically tends toward the irresponsible . . . . Hence, while defying categorization, this public may be considered "attentively passive" toward world affairs.

At this bottom end of the international scale is a third public:

composed basically of the grammar-school-educated and unskilled workers; farmers usually, and skilled workers frequently, are also in it. This public is characterized by low levels of international information and concern, sluggish opinion reactions to events, and unstable and exceedingly pessimistic appraisals of foreign affairs. With little true comprehension of world circumstances, persons in this public rely on stereotypes and prejudice for guidance; their abiding but ill-defined sense of insecurity is amplified to frustration and anxiety by international events compelling their attention. . . .[56]

Another, later, and more general commentary on the effects of formal education is that of Stephens and Long. They say:

... the evidence is respectable, if not maximally strong, that schooling exerts a broad, general influence on a variety of political-behavior variables — *information* on and *interest* in public affairs, *political tolerance, internationalist* outlook, *political participation,* lack of *prejudice,* antimilitarist attitudes, and *generalized liberalism* — with the evidence being stronger for the first five of these than for the last three. With respect to *economic conservatism* we draw no conclusion.[57]

Whether education is more or less important than income and occupation as an indicator of political participation is not apparent as yet. After reviewing much of the literature, Lane concludes:

Perhaps for a simple conventional act such as voting, income is more important, while more complex forms of participation are more dependent upon qualities associated with education. Occupation is hard to grade along a similar, single-dimensional continuum, but from inspection of the 1952 Survey Research Center data, it is apparent (for what it is worth) that differences among standard occupational classifications are smaller than differences among the educational or income classifications.[58]

In view of what we know about the correlations of education with information holding, sense of efficacy, and participation in the opinion-policy process, it is tempting to believe that social improvements might be understood and welcomed by the masses if they only knew more. It is part of the liberal mythology that "education" is a way to get rid of wars, economic dislocations, social injustices, political conflicts, and most of the real and imagined evils attending the human adventure. We have seen enough, even in this brief overview, perhaps, to conclude that the simplistic notion of education as a panacea for social ills is, like most simplistic notions, a fraud. In the first place, a good deal of what is labeled education is no more than public relations — which, as Almond points out, will not do:

It is a great temptation to attribute these differences in political attitudes which are associated with income, occupation, and education to "lack of information" or "areas of ignorance." The policy implications of such an interpretation are clean and simple. Lack of information can be remedied by more information; and "areas of ignorance" can be dispelled by civic-minded campaigns of public education. In actuality, the problem runs a great deal deeper. A discriminating analysis of the evidence suggests that a large sector of the lower-income, poorly educated majority of the population is incapable of assimilating the materials of informational campaigns. Its basic apathy is a consequence of emotional and social conditions. Its intellectual horizon tends to be quite limited, and its analytical skill rudimentary. It will take a great deal more than public relations to remedy such a situation and produce the degree of involvement and activism which is characteristic of the upper-educational and -income groups. Actually, no one has proposed a solution to this basic problem which is not transparently inadequate or obviously Utopian.[59]

It is hard to reach a balanced judgment on the long-run (or even the shorter-run) effects of education on political opinions and behavior. The voice of pessimism is heard in the Almond quotation above. John Kenneth Galbraith, on the other hand, is more hopeful; he argued in 1967 that "a superior and independent education" could provide the individual and social skepticism, and the pluralistic perspectives, to relieve the harsh demands of a superrational industrial system.[60]

It is true that we have little evidence that even small numbers of people can be brought suddenly and lastingly into the ways of democratic participation through the influence of formal and institutionalized education. Mass opinions or behavior cannot be changed in any short period of time; educators can be only slightly in advance of the society which they must reflect as they help to re-create. Change is slow.

Nonetheless, there is some change, and opinions change more quickly than attitudes and beliefs. This may be especially true of opinions that are unrelated to personal experience. Thus in the matter of foreign policy, so critical to the preservation of the evolving welfare democracy in America, mass opinions may be decisively altered by bold and imaginative leadership.

Some of this change is due to the fact that education does widen horizons, and to the fact that in America ever greater numbers are obtaining ever greater education. The attentive public is increasing, not just absolutely, as the population grows, but relative to the size of the inattentive.[61]

This changing ratio means not only that policy issues may receive more discriminating consideration, but that the pool that produces opinion leaders and decisionmakers will be correspondingly larger.[62] Talent for creating and leading public opinion is thus being saved and produced.

Notes:

[1] Alexander L. George and Juliette L. George, *Woodrow Wilson and Colonel House* (New York: The John Day Company, Inc. 1956); Erik H. Erikson, *Young Man Luther* (New York: W. W. Norton & Co., Inc., 1958). For a somewhat more general psychoanalytical study of radical leaders see E. Victor Wolfenstein, *The Revolutionary Personality: Lenin, Trotsky, Gandhi* (Princeton, N.J.: Princeton University Press, 1967).

[2] Allan W. Wicker, "Attitudes vs. Actions: The Relationship of Verbal and Overt Behavioral Responses to Attitude Objects," *Journal of Social Issues,* XXV, No. 4 (1969), 41-78, quote at p. 75. For a good collection of studies and commentaries, see Irwin Deutscher, *What We Say/What We Do: Sentiments and Acts* (Glenview, Ill.: Scott, Foresman and Company, 1973).

[3] Gabriel A. Almond and Sidney Verba, *The Civic Culture: Political Attitudes and Democracy in Five Nations* (Princeton, N.J.: Princeton University Press, 1963), p. 5.

[4] Daniel J. Elazar, *Cities of the Prairie: The Metropolitan Frontier and American Politics* (New York: Basic Books, Inc., 1970), pp. 258-9.

[5] *Ibid.,* p. 264.

[6] Edward Zigler and Irvin L. Child, "Socialization," in G. Lindzey and E. Aronson, eds., *Handbook of Social Psychology,* Vol. III, (Reading, Mass.: Addison-Wesley Publishing Company, Inc., 1969), pp. 450-589.

[7] This definition and the next two quotations are from Kenneth P. Langton, *Political Socialization* (New York: Oxford University Press, 1969), p. 5. Students of political socialization will find a most valuable aid in Jack Dennis, *Political Socialization Research: A Bibliography* (Beverly Hills, Calif.: Sage Publications, 1973).

[8] Charles F. Andrain, *Children and Civic Awareness: A Study in Political Education* (Columbus, Ohio: Charles E. Merrill Publishing Co., 1971), especially Chapter Four, "The Public Philosophy of Children," pp. 41-55.

[9] "The family accounted for almost four times more movement along the entire efficacy scale than either the peer group or school. In fact, it was the only agency that moved students along the whole range of the efficacy scale." — Kenneth P. Langton and David A. Karns, "The Relative Influence of the Family, Peer Group, and School in the Development of Political Efficacy," *Western Political Quarterly,* XXII (December 1969), 922. Niemi says there is little *conscious* political socialization by parents, and most children are "left quite free to develop their own feelings." — Richard G. Niemi, *How Family Members Perceive Each Other: Political and Social Attitudes in Two Generations* (New Haven, Conn.: Yale University Press, 1974), quotation at p. 197.

[10] Bernard Berelson *et al., Voting* (Chicago: University of Chicago Press, 1954), pp. 89, 92. Factor analysis in a panel study of value climates in ten Illinois high schools indicated that the nuclear family influence explained 68 percent of the variations in the party preferences of the students. See Martin L. Levin, "Social Climates and Political Socialization," *Public Opinion Quarterly,* XXIV (1960), 515.

[11] See also Richard E. Dawson, "Political Socialization," in James A. Robinson, ed., *Political Science Annual 1966* (Indianapolis: The Bobbs-Merrill Company, Inc., 1966), pp. 1-84; Fred I. Greenstein, *Children and Politics* (New Haven, Conn.: Yale University Press, 1965); and Richard E. Dawson and Kenneth Prewitt, *Political Socialization* (Boston: Little, Brown & Company, 1968).

[12] R. W. Connell, "Political Socialization in the American Family: The Evidence Re-Examined," *Public Opinion Quarterly,* XXXVI (Fall 1972), 323-33, 330. On sociological (and psychocultural) explanations, see the excellent article by Joseph Adelson, "The Political Imagination of the Young Adolescent," *Daedalus,* C (Fall 1971), 1,013-50. See also Andrew M. Greeley, "A Model for Ethnic Political Socialization," *American Journal of Political Science,* XIX (May 1975), 187-206.

[13] Environmental pressures may overcome family influence quite early, even on the question of party preference. Johnson reports that in rural Kentucky, among young people whose parents supported the minority party locally, from half to two-thirds had defected to the majority party by the time they were 18. — Norris R. Johnson, "Political Climates and Party Choice of High School Youth," *Public Opinion Quarterly,* XXXVI (1972), 48-55.

[14] See Harmon Zeigler, *The Political World of the High School Teacher* (Eugene, Oreg.: Center for the Advanced Study of Educational

Administration, 1966), pp. 8-11, and Ralph Segalman, "The Protestant Ethic and Social Welfare," *Journal of Social Issues,* XXIV (January 1968), 125-41, for personality descriptions and correlates of the Protestant ethic.

[15] Max Weber, *The Protestant Ethic and the Spirit of Capitalism* (New York: Charles Scribner's Sons, 1958), and R.H. Tawney, *Religion and the Rise of Capitalism* (New York: Harcourt, Brace & World, Inc., 1926).

[16] Leonard Goodwin, *Do The Poor Want to Work? — A Social Psychological Study of Work Orientation* (Washington, D.C.: The Brookings Institution, 1972).

[17] Robert Lane, *Political Ideology: Why the American Common Man Believes What He Does* (New York: The Free Press, 1962), pp. 373-7.

[18] See Alexander L. George and Juliette L. George, *Woodrow Wilson and Colonel House* (New York: John Day and Company, Inc., 1956).

[19] Milton Viorst, "Incidentally, Who *Is* Dean Rusk," in Robert Paul Wolff, ed., *Styles of Political Action in America* (New York: Random House, 1972), p. 176.

[20] Raymond E. Wolfinger *et al.,* "America's Radical Right: Politics and Ideology," in David E. Apter, ed., *Ideology and Discontent* (New York: The Free Press, 1964), pp. 281-2. The quote in Item 3 is from David Danzig, "The Radical Right and the Rise of the Fundamentalist Minority," *Commentary,* XXXIII (April 1962), 292.

[21] Samuel Stouffer, *Communism, Conformity and Civil Liberties* (Garden City, N.Y.: Doubleday & Company, Inc., 1955), pp. 146, 148, 155, 203, 205.

[22] *Ibid.,* p. 142.

[23] Merton P. Strommen *et al., A Study of Generations* (Minneapolis: Augsburg Publishing House, 1972), p. 95. Other data *passim.*

[24] Stouffer, *op. cit.,* pp. 143, 151.

[25] Angus Campbell and Homer C. Cooper, *Group Differences in Attitudes and Votes: A Study of the 1954 Congressional Election* (Ann Arbor: Survey Research Center, University of Michigan, 1956), pp. 138, 142.

[26] Lawrence H. Fuchs, *The Political Behavior of American Jews* (New York: The Free Press, 1956), p. 107. Copyright 1956. Reprinted by permission of The Macmillan Company.

[27] *Ibid.,* p. 178.

[28] "Solid evidence of Lutheran preference for the Republican Party is revealed by comparing their voting record in the 1968 presidential

election with the actual results. Whereas Nixon had 1 percent more votes nationally than did Humphrey, Lutherans gave to Nixon 34 percent more votes than they gave to Humphrey. Regional analysis showed that Nixon outdrew Humphrey in Lutheran support by 27 percent in Humphrey's home territory (West, North, Central), and by 43 percent in New England. . ." — Strommen *et al., op. cit.,* p. 46.

[29] Bernard Berelson *et al., Voting* (Chicago: University of Chicago Press, 1954).

[30] Philip E. Converse, "Religion and Politics: The 1960 Election," in Angus Campbell *et al.,* eds., *Elections and the Political Order* (New York: John Wiley & Sons, Inc., 1966), pp. 96-124.

[31] Harry M. Scoble and Leon D. Epstein, "Religion and Wisconsin Voting in 1960," *The Journal of Politics,* XXVI (1964), 396.

[32] Mark R. Levy and Michael S. Kramer, *The Ethnic Factor: How America's Minorities Decide Elections* (New York: Simon and Schuster, 1973), p. 237. Table 4-1 is from the same source. The rows do not add to 100 percent.

[33] Benjamin B. Ringer and Charles Y. Glock, "The Political Role of the Church as Defined by Its Parishioners," *Public Opinion Quarterly,* XVIII (1954), 338.

[34] Strommen *et al., op. cit.,* pp. 377-8. In early 1974 it was asserted that in New York City "the secrecy that was once the trademark of the relationship between clergy and politicians . . . has been replaced by overt political lobbying." — Murray Schumach, "Clergy's Political Power Rises," *New York Times,* January 28, 1974.

[35] Jules Henry, *Culture against Man* (New York: Random House, Inc., 1963), p. 287.

[36] Richard DeCharms and Gerald H. Moeller, "Values Expressed in American Children's Readers: 1900-1950," *Journal of Abnormal and Social Psychology,* LXIV (February 1962), 136-42.

[37] Charles E. Merriam, *Civic Education in the United States* (New York: Charles Scribner's Sons, 1934), p. 77. For some comments on nationalistic distortions in European and American schools and on UNESCO's efforts to reduce such distortions, see Elton Atwater, Kent Forster, and Jan S. Prybyla, *World Tensions: Conflict and Accommodation* (New York: Appleton-Century-Crofts, Inc., 1967), pp. 28-30.

[38] Kenneth P. Langton, "Peer Group and School and the Political Socialization Process," *American Political Science Review,* LXI (September 1967), 751-8.

[39]Robert D. Hess and Judith V. Torney, *The Development of Political Attitudes in Children* (Chicago: Aldine Publishing Co., 1967).

[40]Lee Sigelman and Jonathan Hantke, "The Relative Impact of Socialization Agents: An Exploratory Study," unpublished manuscript, 1974. See also M. Kent Jennings and Richard G. Niemi, *The Political Character of Adolescence: The Influence of Families and Schools* (Princeton, N.J.: Princeton University Press, 1974), especially pp. 319-29.

[41]H. H. Remmers, "Propaganda in the Schools — Do the Effects Last?" *Public Opinion Quarterly*, II (1938), 202.

[42]Dean Jaros, *Socialization to Politics* (New York: Praeger Publishers, 1973), p. 100.

[43]David Easton and Robert D. Hess, "The Child's Political World," *Midwest Journal of Political Science*, VI (August 1962), 236 and 238.

[44]Charles F. Andrain, *Children and Civic Awareness: A Study in Political Education* (Columbus, Ohio: Charles E. Merrill Publishing Co., 1971). Andrain asked the children about the basis for "describing Americans," levels of political tolerance, symbols of national identity, and what made them most proud to live in America. By and large, these 10- and 13-year-olds seem to base their political feelings and beliefs, and even their sense of national identity, on civil rules, norms, and institutions rather than on the primordial values of blood, language, and soil, or sacred values of eternal texts and doctrine.

[45]*Ibid.*, p. 76.

[46]See Kenneth P. Langton and M. Kent Jennings, "Political Socialization and the High School Civics Curriculum," *American Political Science Review*, LXII (September 1968), 852-67.

[47]Edgar Litt, "Civic Education, Community Norms, and Political Indoctrination," *American Sociological Review*, XXVIII (February 1963), 69-75.

[48]Richard M. Merelman, *Political Socialization and Educational Climates: A Study of Two School Districts* (New York: Holt, Rinehart and Winston, Inc., 1971), pp. 105-6.

[49]Kenneth P. Langton, *Political Socialization* (New York: Oxford University Press, 1969), Chapter Six, "Influence of Different Agencies in Political Socialization," pp. 140-60.

[50]Dean Jaros, *op. cit.*, pp. 116-7.

[51]Angus Campbell, G. Gurin, and Warren E. Miller, *The Voter Decides* (New York: Harper & Row, Inc., 1954), p. 187.

[52] Angus Campbell *et al., The American Voter* (New York: John Wiley & Sons, Inc., 1960), p. 280.

[53] Robert E. Agger, Marshall N. Goldstein, and Stanley Pearl, "Political Cynicism: Measurement and Meaning," *The Journal of Politics,* XXIII (1961), 484.

[54] *Ibid.,* 487.

[55] The Oregon investigators divided the notion of political confidence into political trust and political potency. Political trust is a positive evaluation of politics and politicians as being relatively clean, no more selfish than most persons, and generally desirable. The sense of political potency is the feeling that individual action is of some use — that is, it is what the Survey Research Center scholars call political efficacy. Though a person might be politically trusting at the same time that he has a sense of political impotence (or be cynical and feel politically potent), the Oregon study found, as one would expect, that cynicism and impotency were usually found in the same person, just as trust and a sense of potency were found together.

[56] Paul A. Smith, "Opinions, Publics, and World Affairs in the United States," *The Western Political Quarterly,* XIV (1961), 709-13.

[57] William N. Stephens and C. Stephen Long, "Education and Political Behavior," in James A. Robinson, ed., *Political Science Annual: An International Review,* Vol. II, 1969 (Indianapolis: Bobbs-Merrill Company, Inc., 1970), p. 15. Italics in original.

[58] Robert E. Lane, *Political Life* (New York: The Free Press, 1959), p. 222. The authors of an early study concluded that "education and SES level seem to have about equal importance in creating and maintaining political interest." Paul F. Lazarsfeld *et al., The People's Choice* (New York: Columbia University Press, 1944), p. 43.

[59] Gabriel A. Almond, *The American People and Foreign Policy* (New York: Frederick A. Praeger, Publisher, 1960), p. 130.

[60] John Kenneth Galbraith, *The New Industrial State* (New York: The New American Library, 1968), pp. 377-85.

[61] See James N. Rosenau, *Citizenship Between Elections: An Inquiry Into the Mobilizable American* (New York: The Free Press, 1974), pp. 67-88. Stephens and Long say that from the microlevel of the individual, correlations between education and tolerant, participatory political behavior may be slight, but viewed "from the vantage point of the political system, the effects appear to be considerable. These 'weak' attitude changes (with greater formal education) add up statistically

to the pattern of correlations we have reviewed, and to elections won and lost, mandates given and withheld — to a major tilting of public opinion." (Stephens and Long, *op. cit.,* p. 25.)

[62] For a sophisticated and penetrating presentation of a number of the foregoing points, see William A. Gamson and Andre Modigliani, "Knowledge and Foreign Policy Opinions: Some Models for Consideration," *Public Opinion Quarterly,* XXX (1966), 187-99.

5 Relearning Opinions: Micro-Processes

This chapter focuses on the specialized communications techniques and interpersonal relationships that are (in most cases, at least) consciously used for the making and remaking of opinions. We undertake now a more microscopic examination of the organization and techniques of opinion creation and transmission — though candor requires me to repeat what you must already be perfectly aware of: namely, that we have, at this time, only the most incomplete knowledge of the dynamics of opinion holding and opinion change.

We are still dealing with public opinion — with views expressed by significant numbers of persons on issues of public importance — but, for maximum clarity of exposition and understanding, we shall have to move back and forth from the aggregate to the individual levels. For example, in trying to understand the relationship between voting and opinions we might suppose that low turnout among poorer people (expressed in probabilities and percentages, the language of aggregate data) is related to low sense of political efficacy (which is a measurement of an individual characteristic). Or, in the analysis of the mass media, we shall consider the correlation of newspaper exposure to issue opinions and candidate choice, and why individuals read what newspapers and what parts of newspapers. We shall try to understand how and why the individual holds what opinions on public questions, and to determine in what proportion the various points of view on an issue are shared by the members of the public created by that issue.

Our concern may be summarily represented by the following diagram:

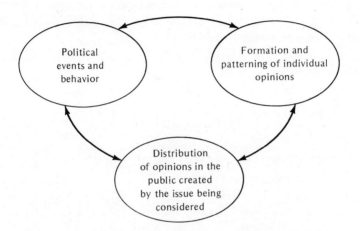

We want to explain political events and behavior. To do so, we need to know something about the politically relevant opinion held by the individual (its cause, intensity, and relation to other opinions); and we need to know about the distribution of that opinion in the mass (i.e., in the public or publics involved).

According to Colin Cherry, communication is "the establishment of a social unit from individuals, by the use of language or signs. [It is] the sharing of common sets of rules, for various goal-seeking activities."[1] At another point, he says communication "is essentially the *relationship* set up by the transmission of stimuli and the evocation of responses."[2]

Human communication needs to be distinghished from animal communication on the basis of its flexibility, its adaptiveness, and its ability to deal with concepts such as space and time. The coinage (more technically, the stimulus) of communication is the "sign"; and signs may be — still in Cherry's terms — languages, codes, or logical-sign systems.

For our purposes, we may say that communication is *the meaningful use of signs to establish social relationships.* In most cases, we may narrow our consideration to language as the stimulus (sign), since, except for the use of gestures and symbols in politics, the currency of communication is the spoken or printed word. More than three thousand languages and dialects are spoken in the world today. Many of these do not have written forms — that is, they do not have conventional visual symbols that represent the sounds of speech and the ideas these sounds convey — and it is likely that there are no more than seventy-five to one hundred languages of importance. But even this number testifies to the flexibility of human invention and the variety of social custom. Chinese is the language spoken by most people, although English is the language most widely spread over the world.

In this book, we deal very largely with communication through language, and with the relationship between small and large communication networks and the holding of opinions on issues of public importance.

PRIMARY GROUPS AND
PRIMARY COMMUNICATION NETWORKS

The sociologist Charles H. Cooley was perhaps the first to recognize the basic distinction between primary and secondary human groups. In 1909 he described primary groups as "those characterized by intimate face-to-face cooperation and association."[3] Homans, a latter-day student of small-group behavior, explicitly added the element of *frequent communication* to the definition of the primary group, which, according to him, is "a number of persons who communicate with each other often over a span of time, and who are few enough so that each person is able to communicate with all the others, not at second-hand, through other people, but face-to-face."[4]

The common definition of the primary group today is a *collection of persons who interact as individuals who are distinguishable, as individuals, from one another.* The dyad, or two-person interaction, is the simplest of these. Work groups, bridge clubs, school classes, and dozens of other ordinary human interactions also constitute primary groups. Cooley's requirement of the members' being face-to-face need not be taken too literally; it is not necessary that the members of a primary group see each other or be in each other's presence. A conference telephone call produces a primary group — and a primary communication network — though the persons may be thousands of miles apart and, except for that particular interaction, total strangers. The only essential ingredients of the primary group, and of the primary communication network, are that the individuals who comprise it shall be recognizable as individuals and that there should be some concerted (probably goal-directed) pattern of activity among them.

Primary groups, and the communication networks established by them, may vary greatly in function, objective, membership, and degree of formality. Some may be wholly and permanently apolitical, some wholly and permanently political, and many with some actual or potential political implications activated at different times and in different degrees.[5]

SECONDARY GROUPS AND
MASS COMMUNICATION NETWORKS

All group relationships in which the members are not recognizable as individuals may be described as *secondary groups*. Categorical groups – for example, all twenty-year-olds or all left-handed males – are one type of secondary group, normally of little concern for anything other than statistical convenience. Our main interest here is what Truman calls *institutionalized groups*, both primary and secondary. Institutionalized groups – the family, organized religion, corporations, civic and fraternal clubs, to give only a few examples – show a rather high degree of formality, uniformity, and generality. Institutionalized groups not of the face-to-face variety are what we choose to call secondary groups.[6] In the analysis of public opinion, we shall use categorical, institutional, and associational secondary groups, in addition to the primary group.

In the marchland between clear-cut primary and secondary groups are some types of human interaction in which individuals may be identifiable as such, with names and significance as persons at some times, but at other times with the individuals lost or merged into the collective whole. The *crowd*, the *assemblage*, and the similar but often distinguished *mob* are terms to conceptualize situations in which the individual, as an individual, may be either visible or submerged in the interaction patterns.

Secondary communication networks can be distinguished from primary communication networks the same way that secondary groups are distinguished from primary groups. Secondary communication networks are mass-communication systems, or simply *mass communication*.

Wright points out that "mass communication is a special kind of communication involving distinctive operating conditions, primary among which are the nature of the audience, of the communication experience, and of the communicator." The audience, he says, is distinguished by its large size, its heterogeneity, and its anonymity; the communication experience is characterized as "public, rapid, and transient"; and the communicator "tends to be, or to operate within, a complex organization that may involve great expense."[7]

The common mass-communication media – the press, radio, television, and the movies – meet all the basic requirements of anonymity, publicness, and institutionalization. They are also more or less rapid and transient, although some parts of each may require considerable time for preparation (e.g., magazine articles and movies) and may in some instances be designed for semipermanent use (e.g., the periodic reissue of old movies). Nevertheless, they are clearly more rapid and transient than such specialized communications as textbooks and scholarly publications, which, at least in theory, have value over an indeterminate span of time.

It will not be profitable for us to try to define each form of communication – especially of printed communications such as pamphlets, newsletters, and memoranda – as mass communication or nonmass. Some may be public, transient, and addressed to a large, heterogeneous audience. Polemical pamphlets and "open letters" to public officials probably should be thought of as mass communication; a diagnostic pamphlet issued by a medical society probably should not. As in all attempts at categorization, some items may not be readily identifiable as mass communications, and can be handled only as they appear. Despite the overlap in practice between mass communication and nonmass forms, the general distinction is important conceptually and has been useful in empirical research.

COMMUNICATION AND DIRECT OBSERVATION AS SOURCES OF OPINION

Opinion formation or change is not necessarily and always the result of communication. Instinct and unaided learning through individual experience may produce some kinds of attitudes and views about some matters. But, as we saw earlier, there can be no opinions worthy of that name without *learning*, and none but the most limited kind of learning without the social relationships that can be established only through communication. Thus, communication is essential to the formation and reformation of those kinds of opinions with which we are concerned.

Members of society get almost all their knowledge of public issues through communication. Each person witnesses directly only a tiny part of the facts and opinions that make up what she knows and thinks about public matters. She sees and hears from others meaningful signs (words and pictures) that help her form or change attitudes and opinions. Some of these messages come from the members of her family, her friends, and others who communicate more or less directly to her; the rest of the messages she receives through impersonal media.

Communication interacts with personal observation. Although very few persons can form or change opinions about public matters without some communication with others, direct observation may supplement, confirm, or disconfirm the meaning of communicated information. Many opinions, formed through communication, are thus tested by personal experience. Information received from primary or mass-communication networks may have convinced medical students A and B that more extensive public welfare services are desirable in their community. As doctors, however, A and B may have very different experiences. If A has many indigent and low-income patients, his experience will no doubt confirm and strengthen his opinion on this issue. If B's patients are drawn largely from persons who can afford private welfare services, B's experience will probably disconfirm her earlier view and may lead to a change of opinion.

There are many ways, at both the individual and group levels, to reduce the conflict and dissonance of communication and observation. Alone, or in groups, we tend to see and hear what we want to see and hear; thus, communication tends to be identical or at least similar to observation. Nevertheless, the interaction of communicated information and directly perceived information, and especially the reconciliation of communication-observation experiences, is an important part of the dynamics of opinion formation and change.

Most opinions are based upon facts or upon other opinions, which are not learned firsthand but are communicated by other individuals. Few opinions are based wholly or, possibly, even in part on direct observation. Moreover, those few that are observation-based are often made possible by conditions that are established by prior communications. When persons think some events or behaviors are important, or when they are especially sensitive and watchful for clues that may give meaning to certain events or behavior, we say these events have *attention salience* for them.

What establishes attention salience? One observation may lead to another or still more observations in a chain of observation: salience — new observation — new salience. If Benjamin Franklin's accounts of his life are to be wholly credited (a matter of controversy among scholars), it was something like this chain that led him from the observation of a kitten's fur to glass-and-wool experiments to the key on the kite and finally to a theory of lightning. The isolated scientist would have no other way to proceed than through ever more well-defined observation-salience-observation cycles. But the progress of science is possible precisely because scientists are not isolated; communication intervenes, and allows great leaps of information accumulation.

So it is also, to a large extent, with all opinion creation and change. Attention salience is created by communication. We learn sometimes by communication what we should, perhaps, be learning by observation.[8] Doctors A and B read in the paper that the President has sent to Congress a proposal for expanded health benefits for the aged. They then pay special attention to need and inadequacy, or to need and adequacy, as real cases appear in their own practices or in the practices of their fellow physicians. Communication — mass communication in this case — creates for them a saliency that leads to direct observation. Or, to take another case, Mr. Oblah has rabidly Protestant parents who first raise his attention-salience to Catholics in politics; he subsequently looks for, and finds, a Catholic party boss in his city. In Oblah's case, primary communication in his family rather than mass communication first triggers his concern. Or, as a final case, the closet academic who becomes a political activist may first through books and scholarly pursuits become aware of social and political problems. What created salience for him (books and academic study) was not clearly either primary or mass communication, but something of both.

THE CREATION AND MAINTENANCE OF GROUP NORMS

Members of self-conscious groups tend to distinguish themselves from nonmembers. Sometimes human groups are formed on the basis of the physical characteristics of their members (men or women, black or white); by place of residence (X community or Y community); by age (under thirty, over sixty-five); by ancestry (Irish, Italian, Mayflowerites); or, most often, probably, on the basis of *shared opinion.* Whatever it is that determines group membership, those who belong have at the outset, or very quickly develop, what Cooley called "we-feeling" and "they-feeling."

Related to we-feeling and whatever common history may exist, and often binding the members together in behavior patterns, are the intangible rules for group identification. These rules are what we know as *group norms* — values, and hierarchies of values, plus behavioral expectations, all frequently unwritten but by no means unimportant in obtaining group objectives and minimizing intragroup conflict. Even the simplest groups possess norms; norms develop in the very act of the creation of a group. They are, in a sense, the unacknowledged and informal codification of the interactions that make group consciousness (we-feeling) possible.

One of the earliest systematic investigations of group behavior was conducted in the Hawthorne, Illinois, plant of the Western Electric Company, makers of telephone equipment. For a rather long period, a team of social psychologists observed the Western Electric employees under various experimental and nonexperimental working conditions. Of the many studies in this series, the experiment of the Bank Wiring Observation Room, briefly described, may illustrate best the way group norms are created — and may illustrate the difficulty of predicting group norms from wholly rational premises.

The Bank Wiring experiment was designed to test some incentive plans based on the view that workers would work harder for extra pay. The workers whose behavior was being studied had been put together in a special room with an observer whose reputed function was to "keep the records." Under varying conditions of extra-pay incentive — much to the investigators' surprise — the workers' production was not significantly changed.

What had happened? Under the circumstances, a special kind of we-feeling had been created among the workers. An informal group had emerged, a group with norms about production output and quotas. This new primary group had evolved a very real understanding, only partly verbalized but, nonetheless, generally accepted. The behavior norms thus created prevented the faster workers from producing more (from being "rate busters"), for fear that management would then reduce the piece-work rate. Likewise, the norms included the expectation that each person would do her share of the work, and that each member would protect these informal agreements from being learned and dealt with by management.[9]

In the Hawthorne studies, group norms had much greater influence, in general, on individual behavior and opinions than did the variables of pay and working conditions, which were directly manipulated by the investigators. Other studies have revealed the importance of the group in the establishment and maintenance of rules of rightness and wrongness and of behavior for members of the group.[10]

Opinion Similarity Within Groups

Depending upon the importance of the group to the individuals who comprise it, the group norms will strongly or weakly influence the shared opinions. The importance of the group to its members will be the result of many personal propensities, views, and judgments. Importance may be measured by various tests of cohesion or integration, one frequent element of which is an index of sameness of opinion among the group members.

Much of the study of political behavior depends on the similarities and dissimilarities of opinion and candidate preference within and among groups. In our consideration of the sociology of opinion holding, we discussed the influence of family, religious, and economic groupings. It was no surprise to find clusterings of political opinions significantly related to group membership; indeed, large-scale analysis of public opinion would be nearly impossible if it could not be demonstrated that people who share group membership tend to hold similar political views.

The extent to which members of groups are aware of the sameness of their views appears to depend on the size of the group, the intensiveness of group interaction in the past, the relevance of the issues for group functioning, and the centrality or marginality of the individual whose judgment is under consideration. In general, and as would be expected, leaders and centrally located members of small, long-established groups are able to assess very accurately the opinions of the group on issues of salience to the group.[11]

The Influence of Group Norms on "Objective" Judgments

No one will be surprised that group members have consistent similarities of opinion. It may be of some interest, however, that group members, under certain conditions, tend to agree with one another on judgments that appear to be purely objective — even when such judgments are erroneous in fact.

The social psychologist Muzafer Sherif discovered that perceptions, as well as opinions, of individuals are influenced by group norms. He was investigating the *autokinetic effect* — the fact that a stationary point of light, viewed through a totally dark box, *appears* to oscillate. He found that reports of the amount of light movement given by individuals in a group setting tended to converge around a group norm. Individuals who first reported greater or lesser movement when alone, tended after discussion to agree with the median reports.[12]

Asch, elaborating on Sherif's methods, systematically varied the intensity and division of opinions with the use of "stooges." He found that the "naive" subjects in a large majority of cases yielded to group pressures to converge on the norms established by the "stooge" subjects at the will of the investigator. He found, among other things, that the "majority effect" attained full strength when three out of four subjects agreed, and that the tendency of a single minority member to yield to the majority position was not changed by increasing the majority.[13]

Group Norms and Opinions on Public Issues

A word of caution is perhaps in order. The pioneering studies of Sherif and Asch, like others carried out in the laboratory, are very dramatic. They illustrate well what is important for our purposes here, namely, the influence of group pressures and expectations on individual opinions. Nevertheless, there is a danger in over-estimating these evidences of the influence of group norms. Olmsted summarizes the dangers of laboratory experiments as:

1. *Generalization from too little information:* "It is evident that these experiments make no claim to have investigated all the possible effects of the group on the individual . . . our knowledge can hardly be said to be very systematic or exhaustive."

2. *Transference from unreal to real situations:* "It is . . . important to ask whether behavior observed in the laboratory and
that observed in the 'real' world are the same in fact or in name
only. . . . The sort of experimentation described above is only
in the broadest sense a study of groups at all. These groups
— or, more accurately, aggregates of subjects — have very little
interaction and almost no organization or structure."

3. *Temptation to explain all behavior in terms of the influence
of groups:* "Third is the danger that 'group norms' become
an explanation for everything. Further exploration of group
behavior can too easily be smothered by the apparently wise
but actually trite explanation of this or that happens because
of a group norm."[14]

Bearing in mind the dangers of overgeneralization from too little or
unreal evidence, the discovery and elaboration of the importance of
small-group—individual relations is one of the most significant developments of modern social science. The influence of small groups on individual members is not, for public questions, that of direct and explicit
norms that are essential to the operation and survival of the group and
that the individual is constrained to observe. Opinions on issues that can
be called public are ordinarily not critical to the smooth functioning of
primary groups. Many families, work groups, and social clubs include
members whose views on public issues differ widely from the average
opinion of the group — this is clearly true; but it is equally true that
there are influences on both the group and the individual whenever there
is even the slightest indication of these opinion differences. One important reason for such influences is the fact that individuals respond to
what they *believe* to be group norms; opinions are formed or held in
accordance with what might be called the *anticipated pressures* from
the group. To test this proposition, Steiner interviewed a national sample
and a local (Michigan) sample for opinions toward the economic and
political power of big business and for the norms these respondents
assumed to be held by their closest friends. He concluded "that perceived primary-group pressures can have considerable effect on attitudes
even when there is reason to doubt that group norms and sanctions are
operating."[15] Thus it appears that we shape our opinions in some political or quasi-political matters on the basis of what we think our group-
friends' views are, even when we don't *know* whether our friends have

any views at all. This is a special application of what Friedrich calls the "rule of anticipated reactions" — that people often behave not on the simple basis of the past, but on their expectations of how others will react to whatever they do.[16]

Whether group norms are known or presumed, it could be argued that the pressure to conform will be greater, not less, in social and political than in other matters. The pressure to conform to the opinions of those around us is strong

> even when there is a clear objective referent for our opinions, but it is more the case with those political and social opinions for which there is no clear and easy test except comparison with the opinions of our fellows. In such testing situations, there is pressure on the individual to change his opinion if it differs from the opinion of others around him. These pressures come both from the individual himself and from the other group members, since the condition of dissonance will be unpleasant to both the deviant and the other group members.[17]

ROLE DIFFERENTIATION IN PRIMARY GROUPS

All members of groups do not perform, for the group, the same kinds of tasks or behave, in group interaction, in identical ways. Individuals in groups have various roles to play. Although there is considerable disagreement about the nuances and specialized meanings of *role* and *role behavior*,[18] one useful and typical statement defines a social role as "an organized pattern of expectancies that relate to the tasks, demeanors, attitudes, values, and reciprocal relationships to be maintained by persons occupying specific membership positions and fulfilling definable functions in any group." In their definition of role, these authors place emphasis "on expectancies rather than behavior, because the role is defined by what others expect of the person filling it. Behavior refers to actual performance — how a person fills his role."[19]

There may be *natural roles*, determined by sex and generational differences, as in the obvious examples of the mother and father roles in the primary family group. In formally organized groups, specialized officers may handle *functional roles* (that is, behavior for facilitating the attainment of group purposes), such as presiding over meetings (the president or chairman), handling group finances (the treasurer), or taking care of group communications (the secretary).

More important to us than the kinds of roles that exist is the evidence that social roles influence opinions about political issues. Many wives find in their wifely role the reasons, or at least the rationalizations, for their disinterest and lack of information about public affairs — "Oh, my husband does the political thinking in our family." It is a belief among junior corporation executives "on the rise" that their role requires them to be inactive in politics and without opinions (at least, without *expressed* opinions) on issues of public concern. Clergymen will not ordinarily express highly political opinions; and even the Pope, whose leadership role for Roman Catholics is broadly defined, speaks infallibly only on matters of faith and morals.

In situations of more highly concentrated politics, social roles heavily influence the nature of opinion creation and exchange. The candidate role carries with it expectations absent from (or even incompatible with) the role expectations of the elected legislator — or, a fortiori, the elected judge.

At less lofty levels, and throughout the opinion-policy process, role considerations bear on the existence and intensity of public opinion. On public finance questions, the bankers are listened to closely; the views of the "Mothers' Committee of Public School 310" are given special attention on education matters; almost any "older businessman" is respected by his younger colleagues when public issues are discussed. In all groups (but in primary groups especially), role considerations bear on opinion formation and change; in some group relationships, role may be insignificant, or nearly so, whereas in others it may be of central importance.

PERSONAL EXPERIENCES
AND PERSONAL INFLUENCE

It is apparent that role is related to experience. The leader has led, the expediter has expedited, and the inside-dopester has acquired inside dope. Conceivably, one could fill a role without gaining experience in the practical matters and specialized knowledge associated with that role; role behavior, to continue Hartley and Hartley's distinction, could be irrelevant to role efficacy. In general, however, there should be a fairly close correspondence between influence associated with role and influence associated with experience. In simple societies — and to some extent in those not so simple — the village elder has a large-group social role as patriarch, which is in turn related to genealogical fact and to his personal experience. His experience supports his role, and his role makes possible an increase in his influence as a leader of opinion.

Role is thus quite obviously related to specialization of labor. Both social role and labor specialization create the presumption of opinion expertise. Plato believed that some people have expert training, skills, and competence and others have none. Whatever the case may have been 2,500 years ago in Greece, a more modern view of society would recognize that specializations — and roles and experience based on specializations — are spread very widely. In the nineteenth century George Cornewall Lewis went beyond the mere fact that specialization of roles and experience means that expert knowledge (and, therefore, reliable opinion) is divided unequally in society. "In considering the seat of authority," Lewis observed, "it should be borne in mind, on the one hand, that no man is a competent judge on *all* subjects; and, on the other, that every man is a competent judge on *some*."[20] The evidence of some recent field studies indicates that Lewis was right. Specialized interest and specialized experience create specialized opinion leadership. Among their more than seven hundred women respondents in Decatur, Illinois, Katz and Lazarsfeld found very few "general" leaders — so few, in fact, that those found might have been the product of interviewing error or dishonest responses.[21] Younger, single women, in the Katz and Lazarsfeld study, had their opinions sought by other women on matters of clothing style and fashion; married women with larger families were sources of general marketing advice; in public affairs, the specialized opinion leaders seemed to be those higher in social status and gregariousness (an index of nonneighbor contacts and group membership).

There appear to be very few general opinion leaders. In nondemocratic polities, general leaders might be accepted on tradition or trained within a ruling caste or class. But modern democratic practice and the diversification of power in social pluralism produce specialized opinion leaders for the most part. Nowadays there are very few "men for all seasons," and it is significant that a great many of the most knowledgeable and participative members of an elite sample thought themselves quite poorly informed on many of the major issues they were asked about in 1964.[22]

Nevertheless, having made the important point that individual leaders, even those of great power, are specialized leaders, we must observe a paradox. It is that government, by its nature as the supreme and ultimate power grouping of modern society, requires executives who give the appearance of general opinion leaders. And the institutional aggregation of specialized opinion leadership makes executive generalization more than a mere appearance. Effective staffing provides the political executive with an array of specialization that, through the device of ministerial responsibility, results in the functional equivalent of general opinion leadership. The President may become, in effect, a general opinion leader by pooling the talents of expert assistants, each of whom has quite limited expertise.[23]

PERSONAL INFLUENCE ON
PUBLIC OPINION FORMATION AND CHANGE

Political scientists and sociologists have only recently rediscovered the importance of person-to-person contact in opinion formation and change. Despite the early writings of Cooley, Mead, and other sociologists, and the significant work of Mayo and other industrial psychologists, it was not until the 1940s and 1950s that the wider implications of primary-group interactions became apparent.

Retrospectively, it seems clear why the effects of primary communication networks were not understood and acknowledged until recently. Before the age of scientific sample surveys, what we knew (or thought we knew) about political behavior was largely gained deductively from "general principles" of human action or empirically from the observation of atypical individuals and groups. In particular, our understanding was limited by two conceptions that we now believe to have been inaccurate or oversimplified. One was, and is, the old bugaboo of "the rational man," the implications of which we have considered at earlier points in this book. We need not repeat here the warnings and dangers of believing that reason and logic control human behavior. We need only say, in this context, that habit, faith, avoidance of commitment (i.e., indifference and apathy), and the other nonrational sources of human behavior often depend on informal — perhaps even unrecognized — person-to-person influences. It is an interesting question, in this age of what Riesman calls "other-directedness," whether the influence of nonrational factors is greater than it was in earlier periods of "inner-directed" social ethic. In any case, reason is only one — and often one of the least important — of the elements that create opinions. Our earlier model of the rational man was too simple; and its simplicity made it easy for us to ignore other influences — among which are the influences of casual friends and neighbors.

In addition to the overemphasis of reason, our earlier views of opinion formation and change presumed that the mass media provided the individual with facts and opinions that were absorbed directly, without the aid of mediation or translation by other individuals. The influence of the mass media was thought to be immediate, direct, and more or less equal in its impact. "In short," as Katz and Lazarsfeld say, "the media of communication were looked upon as a new kind of unifying force — a simple kind of nervous system — reaching out to every eye and ear, in a society characterized by an amorphous social organization and a paucity of interpersonal relations.[24]

The influence of the mass media is not so simple. Not all persons are equally or randomly exposed to mass media, and people therefore receive different messsages. Programming varies from medium to medium and within each medium — another factor accounting for variety in what individuals receive from mass communications. Furthermore, people seem to seek out from the mass media information that they believe will be particularly useful for the conversations they anticipate having.[25] Finally, individuals who receive the very same messages find different meanings in them, depending upon what they are or are not looking for and upon what information and skill they have in relating these messages to other messages.

These disturbing complexities led a number of analysts to differentiate individuals (to take them out of the "mass") according to the roles they played in the flow of information and opinions. The authors of *The People's Choice*, first among survey researchers, "discovered" that some people are, in Orwell's celebrated phrase, "more equal than others" when it comes to determining the way votes will be cast. Personal influence, they found, was probably more important than formal media in determining voting decisions. Personal contact is apt to reach persons not exposed to media messages. Not only is personal influence more extensive than mass-media political influence, but, as the authors of this pioneer study point out, personal influence has the following psychological advantages:

1. *It is nonpurposive:* "politics gets through, especially to the indifferent . . . because it comes up unexpectedly as a sideline or marginal topic in a casual conversation."
2. *It is flexible when countering resistance:* "can counter and dislodge such resistance . . . can make use of a large number of cues . . . can choose the occasion at which to speak . . . can adapt [the] story to . . . the other's interests and his ability to understand."
3. *It offers immediate reward for compliance:* "When someone yields to a personal influence in making a vote decision, the reward is immediate and personal. This is not the case in yielding to an argument via print or radio [or television]."
4. *It allows the individual to put his trust in a known and intimate source:* "The doubtful voter . . . can trust the judgment and evaluation of the respected people among his associates. Most of them are people with the same status and interests as himself. Their attitudes are more relevant for him than the judgments of an unknown editorial writer."
5. *It allows for persuasion without conviction:* "Personal influence, with all its overtones of personal affection and loyalty, can bring to the polls votes that would otherwise not be cast or would be cast for the opposing party just as readily if some other friend had insisted. [It] differs from the formal media by persuading uninterested people to vote in a certain way without giving them a substantive reason for their vote."[26]

The power of personal influence to induce *behavior* for what are essentially irrelevant reasons is not found to the same degree in the mass media. Most of the strength of personal influence lies in the willingness of individuals to think or do things simply because their friends want them to.

In the 1950s and 1960s it was common for communications researchers to talk about what they called the "two-step flow" of information and opinions. The inventors of the term said that "ideas often flow *from* radio and print *to* opinion leaders and *from* them to the less active sections of the population."[27] By 1961 it could be claimed that "this so-called two-step flow hypothesis has been used in several studies and with modification, is probably the most popular framework, explicitly or implicitly, utilized in diffusion research."[28]

It is, no doubt, an oversimplification that there are usually only two steps in the spread of information or opinions from mass media to individual consumer.[29] Very often there seem to be many steps. For the knowledge and activity of opinion leaders are qualified, of course, by many other considerations, of which socioeconomic status, education, personality characteristics (e.g., gregariousness), role, and ego-involvement are important. But the overall pattern appears to be that of multi-dimensional networks of opinion giving and opinion taking in which the opinion givers are (a) *many* – although some never seem to have their views sought, or accepted if volunteered; (b) *specialized* – although "general" opinion leaders may exist in some communities and at some social levels; and (c) *effective* (insofar as they are effective) to some considerable degree through informal and unself-conscious techniques of conversation and example-setting.

Much remains to be learned about influence and the transfer of opinions through primary- and small-group communication. It seems probable – although the evidence is not yet available – that the essentially private matters studied by most sociologists in small-group research (and to a large degree by Katz and Lazarsfeld in their interviews with the women of Decatur) are heavily influenced by the primary-group contacts each person experiences in day-to-day living. An individual's opinions about public questions seem to be less influenced by peers than by the strata of people immediately above him, to whom he turns for information and (perhaps, more often) conclusions that square in some general way with (a) his own basic attitudes and (b) the values of those primary groups to which he feels allegiance. For public questions, the governmental and group leaders, the managers and producers of the mass media, and others who are visible or powerful in the hierarchies of social institutions (churches, schools) – these people, whom Almond, Roper, and Rosenau describe, will be more important sources of opinions than mere friends and acquaintances. It is to these larger leaders, and their use of mass-communications media, that we now turn in the next chapter.

Notes:

[1]Colin Cherry, *On Human Communication*, 2d ed. (Cambridge, Mass.: Science Editions, Inc., 1966), p. 303.

[2]*Ibid.*, p. 7. Italics in original.

[3]Charles H. Cooley, *Social Organization* (New York: Charles Scribner's Sons, 1909), p. 23.

[4]George C. Homans, *The Human Group* (New York: Harcourt, Brace & World, Inc., 1950), p. 1.

[5]See Sidney Verba, *Small Groups and Political Behavior* (Princeton, N.J.: Princeton University Press, 1961), especially pp. 3-60, for an excellent statement and overview of the importance of primary groups and politics.

[6]David B. Truman, *The Governmental Process* (New York: Alfred A. Knopf, Inc., 1951), pp. 26-7. Truman's attention is focused on political-interest groups, and especially on "associations," which he describes as groups that grow out of "tangent relations" with institutionalized groups (pp. 33-41).

[7]Charles R. Wright, *Mass Communication: A Sociological Perspective* (New York: Random House, Inc., 1959), p. 13-5.

[8]For some stimulating, and even quite revolutionary, propositions about the human capacity to gain and hold knowledge, see Michael Polanyi, *Personal Knowledge: Towards a Post-Critical Philosophy* (Chicago: University of Chicago Press, 1958); and, by the same author, *The Study of Man* (Chicago: University of Chicago Press, 1959).

[9]For the Hawthorne studies, see F. J. Roethlisberger and William J. Dickson, *Management and the Worker* (Cambridge, Mass.: Harvard University Press, 1939).

[10]See, for example, William F. Whyte, *Street Corner Society* (Chicago: University of Chicago Press, 1943); and Henri Tajfel, "Social and Cultural Factors in Perception," in G. Lindzey and E. Aronson, eds., *Handbook of Social Psychology,* 2d ed., Vol. III (Reading, Mass.: Addison-Wesley Publishing Company, 1969), pp. 335-9.

[11]For a helpful summary of findings, see Harold H. Kelley and John W. Thibaut, "Group Problem Solving," in G. Lindzey and E. Aronson, eds., *Handbook of Social Psychology*, 2d ed., Vol. IV (Reading, Mass.: Addison-Wesley Publishing Company, Inc., 1969), pp. 1-101.

[12]Muzafer Sherif, "Group Influences upon the Formation of Norms and Attitudes," in Eleanor E. Maccoby et al., *Readings in Social*

Psychology (New York: Holt, Rinehart and Winston, Inc., 1958), pp. 219-32.

[13] Solomon E. Asch, "Effects of Group Pressure upon the Modification and Distortion of Judgments," in H. Guetzkow, ed., *Groups, Leadership and Men* (Pittsburgh: Carnegie Press, 1951), pp. 177-90.

[14] Michael S. Olmsted, *The Small Group* (New York: Random House, Inc., 1959), p. 76.

[15] Ivan D. Steiner, "Primary Group Influences on Public Opinion," *American Sociological Review*, XIX (1954), 267.

[16] Carl J. Friedrich, *Man and His Government: An Empirical Theory of Politics* (New York: McGraw-Hill Book Company, Inc., 1963), pp. 203-6. The "rule of anticipated reactions" does not reduce the importance of personal or social history, because our anticipations of the future reactions of significant others must be based on our projections of their reactions to similar events of the past. In order to figure out what they will probably do in the future, we have to know what they have done in like situations in the past.

[17] Sidney Verba, *Small Groups and Political Behavior* (Princeton University Press, 1961), pp. 23-4. Verba cites Leon Festinger, *A Theory of Cognitive Dissonance* (Stanford, Calif.: Stanford University Press, 1957).

[18] See Lionel J. Neiman and James W. Hughes, "The Problem of the Concept of Role — A Re-Survey of the Literature," *Social Forces*, XXX (1951), 141-9.

[19] Eugene L. Hartley and Ruth E. Hartley, *Fundamentals of Social Psychology* (New York: Alfred A. Knopf, Inc., 1952), p. 486.

[20] George Cornewall Lewis, *An Essay on the Influence of Authority in Matters of Opinion* (London: Longmans, Green, 1875), p. 114; italics in original. The work was first published in 1849.

[21] Elihu Katz and Paul F. Lazarsfeld, *Personal Influence* (New York: The Free Press, 1955), p. 334. However, a reassessment of Katz and Lazarsfeld's material led two scholars to the conclusion that generalized opinion leaders existed among the Decatur women. See Alan S. Marcus and Raymond A. Bauer, "Yes: There Are Generalized Opinion Leaders," *Public Opinion Quarterly*, XXVIII (1964), 628-32.

[22] James N. Rosenau, *Citizenship Between Elections* (New York: The Free Press, 1974), pp. 346-9. See also Everett M. Rogers, *Diffusion of Innovations* (New York: The Free Press, 1961), pp. 236-7.

[23] Legislative bodies also, but not so effectively, rely for overall competence on the interdependent expertise of their individual members and staffs.

[24] Katz and Lazarsfeld, *op. cit.*, p. 16.

[25] See Charles K. Atkin, "Anticipated Communication and Mass Media Information Seeking," *Public Opinion Quarterly*, XXXVI (1972), 188-99, for evidence on this point and for a review of earlier studies.

[26] Paul F. Lazarsfeld *et al., The People's Choice*, 2d ed. (New York: Columbia University Press, 1948), pp. 152-6.

[27] *Ibid.*, p. 151. Italics in original.

[28] Rogers, *op. cit.*, p. 213. For a review of much of the literature on two-step flow research, see Everett Rogers and Floyd Shoemaker, *Communication of Innovation* (New York: Free Press, 1971). And for a comment on two-step flow theory from the viewpoint of the sociology of knowledge, see Leon Bramson, *The Political Context of Sociology* (Princeton, N.J.: Princeton University Press, 1961), Chapter Five.

[29] In 1968 a panel of Milwaukee voters perceived the media as being of more direct importance (for voting decisions) than "immediate family" or "close friends." — *Media and Non-Media Effects on the Formation of Public Opinion* (Washington, D.C.: The American Institute for Political Communication, 1969), p. 14.

6 Relearning Opinions : Macro-Processes

To this point we have considered some of the important factors, causal and influential, that shape opinions in individuals and, through individuals, in groups. We have considered the influence of culture (patterns of thought and behavior that are approved and disapproved), and of larger social institutions, such as family, religion, and economic organization. Now we shall deal with the way human communication binds individuals together and makes possible meaningful opinion interaction in a social context. Here we are concerned with *mass communication*.

Mass communications are made through the mass media. The mass media, in order of importance for public opinion, are: the press, television, radio, and movies. By the press I mean, first, newspaper, and, second, news and opinion journals. Family magazines, women's magazines, picture magazines such as *People*, and other periodicals of fiction and entertainment are, of course, part of the American press. No doubt, articles in a popular potpourri like *Reader's Digest* have some influence on the underlying predispositions of American voters. For the most part, however, the printed word that is important in American politics appears in the newspapers and in a few weekly or monthly journals, such as *Time, Newsweek, U.S. News & World Report, Harper's, Fortune,* and *Atlantic*, and in a few smaller journals, such as *Commentary, America, National Review,* and *The New Republic*.

MAJOR INFLUENCES OF THE
MASS MEDIA ON PUBLIC OPINION

One of the elements of American political folklore is that the mass media, especially the newspapers, have great influence over the course of elections, legislation, and executive decisions. This bit of "common knowledge" is especially cherished by defeated candidates and reformist interest groups who find some comfort in the identification of scapegoats for the failures of their causes. But winners and status quo organizations also subscribe in large measure to the view that the mass media can move political mountains.

There are some valid reasons why the mass media are felt to be powerful influences in the political dialogue and in the political resolution of social conflict. One is that the mass media do, indeed, influence political decisions – by giving, or withholding, publicity (and, sometimes, endorsements) to candidates and promoters of policy, and (through their editorializing) by helping a small number of people make up their minds about issues. Another reason the media are politically important is quite simply that political decisionmakers often *think* they are important. If enough people whose collective influence is great think that the *New York Times* editorials are important, or that the CBS and NBC public affairs "specials" are powerful expressions of concern and of popular value judgments, then these media presentations do become influential – but more because of what they are thought to be than because of what they are.

In part, this escalation of importance occurs with regard to the mass media because there are so few ostensibly impartial indicators of what people think about public policy. Special-interest pleading there is aplenty; but there are not many ways for the attentive decisionmaker to find out "what the people *really* think." The tendency is for political actors to believe that the mass media somehow have special insight into the "public mind" (an illusion carefully nurtured by the self-image of the press).

Despite their giant-killing reputation among politicians, the mass media are not powerful and merciless defenders or destroyers of the good society. Their influence is, in most cases, less than overwhelming, never monolithic (an important point, to which we will return in a later chapter), and often inconsequential.

Most Mass Media Are Not Very Political. To keep a perspective on the political significance of the mass media, we should bear in mind that the media are, to a very large degree, apolitical — if not antipolitical. Why do newspapers, TV and radio stations, movies, journals, and mass-circulation books exist? For one thing, they exist to make money for their owners and producers — another important matter to which we shall return later in this book. From the perspective of the consumer, however, the mass media provide three main functions: (a) entertainment; (b) a guide and orientation for daily living; and (c) a source of information and opinion about public events. Of these three functions, it is undeniable that the third is least important for the majority of media consumers. Much of the intellectuals' criticism of the mass media misses this simple point: *Most mass-media consumers neither want nor appreciate the subtleties of political discourse.* Moreover, for those who are politically aware and active, the mass media provide only a part of the environment of influence.

Some Media Are More Political Than Others. Great differences exist in the way media spokesmen interpret their public responsibilities. The history and traditions of the medium tend to shape the self-image of its social function. Motion picture producers are fond of telling congressional committees that Hollywood's job is to entertain people, not to teach them civic virtues or political philosophy. The great Sam Goldwyn himself is supposed to have said to an idealistic young screen writer: "If you want to send messages, use Western Union."

Television and radio spokesmen have traditionally viewed their media in much the same apolitical way that movie manufacturers see Hollywood's responsibilities. But the history, and therefore the traditions, of public accountability in radio and TV are somewhat different from that of movies. Movies do not depend, as do TV and radio, on a scientific fact which from the very beginning made regulation of the airwaves a matter of public necessity. The materials for making and showing movies are widely distributed and practically unlimited. But only a small number of radio transmission bands exist, and their rational use required early and continued governmental regulation at the national and international levels. Yet radio and TV — regulated by government because they were, in the words of Chief Justice Waite, "affected by a public interest"— nevertheless resisted political involvement; TV and radio stations do relatively little editorializing, even though they have been free to do so since 1949.

Audiences Do Not Want the Media to Be Very Political. Audiences, too, resist the "public service" programming required of TV and radio stations. As television became available to more and more families from 1947 to 1957, it gradually replaced radio and the movies as the major source of entertainment for almost all categories of Americans. By the end of 1957, three-fourths of a national sample declared television their main source of entertainment. The electronic media are seen as part of the "fun" of the ordinary day – like the comic strip of the newspaper and the lunchtime chatter of bench- or officemates. As Alfred Hero says, "It appears that television and, to a declining extent, radio, are accepted as part of the daily routine, a reward of pleasure built into daily cycles of work and relaxation. At the end of a day's labor, most citizens seek entertainment, not the additional work involved in absorbing new information and ideas."[1] About 85 percent of the content of commercial TV and radio stations consists of entertainment or of advertising related to an entertainment program. In view of these propensities of Americans, and in view of the fingertip availability of TV entertainment, it is not surprising that the average set is turned on for an estimated six hours each day. Nor is it surprising that those who are heavy users of TV seem to be very conventional in attitudes and in social and political opinions.[2]

THE MEDIA AS POLITICAL AGENDA-SETTERS

Although the media are not primarily political in their social significance, and despite the limited political tolerance of mass audiences, the newspapers and, increasingly, television news and public affairs departments have much influence on what issues get considered in American state and national politics. This may sound like a paradox, but it is not. The major daily newspapers and TV network (and large urban independent) news departments are the main channels for the democratic dialogue in all political communities of size. Activist groups and their speakers can suggest, demand, implore, deplore, and confront, but their efforts will fail unless the newspapers and television pay attention to them. The wizards of public relations may plan and scheme, and may "float" or "balloon up" endless ideas, but their skills are for naught unless the city desk or the nightly news takes note. When an issue is picked up by the papers and TV news, then a serious and sustained dialogue *may* take place, but if that is to happen political opinion leaders of several kinds must respond and react, charge and countercharge. And as long as that clash of elites continues to reinforce and to be reinforced by the media presentations, the issue will be under consideration. Later I shall discuss the process of policy-making and policy-changing, of which the agenda-setting aspects are only a part.

Here it is enough to observe that the major daily newspapers and the TV news departments exercise great power in American politics by virtue of their ability to emphasize, specify, and focus on certain issues, and thereby escalate them into importance for the whole polity. "In choosing and displaying news, editors, newsroom staff, and broadcasters play an important part in shaping political reality. Readers learn not only about a given issue, but also how much importance to attach to that issue from the amount of information in a news story and its position. In reflecting what candidates are saying during a campaign, the mass media may well determine the important issues — that is, the media may set the 'agenda' of the campaign."[3]

THE COMMON DENOMINATOR
IN MASS-MEDIA PROGRAMMING

Although the mass media generally do not regard themselves as political phenomena — and although audiences do not want them to be or become such — political leaders (for reasons we have hinted at) *think* the mass media to be (a) highly political, and (b) politically very important. These are, for our purposes, the two most significant characteristics of the mass media.

However, there are other characteristics that have importance for the opinion-policy process. Some of these have to do with the fact that the audiences of the mass media are unknown, in the most complete meaning of the word *unknown* — they are without personality; they are nonpersons, except in a statistical sense. Consequently, mass media programs cannot focus beyond the most general interests — or, perhaps a better way of saying it, beyond the average audience member's tolerance either for specificity or abstraction. Thus, "situation comedy," as the phrase goes, is the most popular kind of TV fare; and the dramatic immorality of celebrities makes the best newspaper copy.

But mass appeal has its price; namely, programming pitched to an anonymous audience, whose common characteristics can be assumed, and catered to, but whose special interests can be neither known nor served.

To counter this disability, the media make many efforts to "personalize" their content, using colloquialisms, first-person address, and ego associations with fictional characters, who are, indeed, typical in their thought processes, but unusual in their dialogue, since they appear clever beyond all commonness. The most successful TV commentators of the intimate genre build up large followings of viewers who sense that these actors, though still actors and still commercial, in some ways and to some degree cut across the common denominator. Such talents, however, have not often been used with avowedly political intentions; and it is doubtful that even the most winningly personalized approach would make television useful for the direct shaping of the political opinions of persons who are generally indifferent to public issues.

We can expect, therefore, that, despite the efforts of the mass media to strike "plain folks" and ego-involving postures, most of the opinion formation of the majority of apolitical citizens will result from person-to-person relationships rather than from direct media-to-person relationships. There is evidence that "specialized media systems" (telephone calls, educational and noncommercial radio stations, postal service, books, suburban newspapers, and legitimate theater) grew faster than the conventional *mass* media from 1947 to 1970. One social scientist at least seems to think that "the mass media will — contrary to past expectations — play a less important role in the future, and the focus of scientific attention should be shifted to specialized media."[4]

CULTURAL PREDISPOSITIONS AND THE MASS MEDIA

We considered the effects of culture on opinions and commented on the fact that opinions are limited by the generally accepted standards of good taste, fairness, and the humanistic traditions of Western culture. We also observed that industrialized societies tend to be characterized by a great diversity of values and behavior standards and that, in contrast to pre-modern societies, the cultural restrictions of the United States in the 1970s are small indeed. Except for the myths that relate to nationalism and patriotism, almost all cultural commands and injunctions can be safely questioned; the range of potential opinion is great; and the limits of public opinion are not to be found so much in cultural prescriptions or proscriptions as in the deficiencies of imagination and in the ego needs that make conformity attractive and nonconformity painful.

Nevertheless, there are some cultural proclivities in twentieth-century America that have importance for the mass media. For one thing, there is a lingering belief that the citizen *ought* to have an opinion on all matters of public policy. The ideal of the omnicompetent citizen has filtered deeply and widely throughout American society, the evidence of which may be found in the answers of survey respondents who say "yes" or "no" when they should say "I don't know," and in the deep contradictions of the New Haven workingmen interviewed by Lane, who were very badly informed but who refused either to blame others for their ignorance or to turn to others for advice. This phenomenon, which Lane has aptly called "the parthenogenesis of knowledge," is a characteristic observed by de Tocqueville in the 1830s and is related to fears of being influenced, as well as to the idea of the "rational" man that is so pervasive in American culture.[5]

Persons who believe — yet not too strongly — that they *ought* to have opinions tend to look to the mass media for help. But because in most people the motivation for opinions on public issues is weak, as the facility for the ordering and assessing of relevant facts also is weak, the help sought from the mass media is in the nature of clues that make public events simple and consistent with pre-existing values and a conventional world view. The mass media are consequently obliged to simplify, dramatize, and emotionalize the reporting of events at the same time they cater to the need for personalization. The reader has his cake and eats it too when he reads a headline that tells him (without his having to be influenced by another person, friend or stranger) briefly and simply that a public event or issue may be thought of within the context of an already existing opinion or set of opinions.

A number of investigators have studied the effects of mass media on the political behavior of Americans. Findings are reviewed in Lane's *Political Life* where the major effects of the mass media on political behavior are summarized as follows:

Exposure to the media increases political discussion, and political discussion increases exposure to the media.

The reinforcement effect of the media is greater than the conversion effect.

While reading, listening, and viewing political material in the media are sometimes substitutes for civic or political action (narcotizing dysfunction), usually they are preliminary to such action.

While the media occasionally discourage political action by featuring the complexity of social problems, more frequently they oversimplify them, giving a (false) impression that the members of the public can devise their own solutions.

The media present more news and comment on public affairs than most of the public demand, thus politicizing rather than apathizing the public.

Failure of the media to establish ideological rapport with large sections of the public tends to discourage participation.

While the news sections of the media tend to give prominence to political figures, and, in this sense, confer status upon them and upon political activity, the fiction in the media fails to cast its heroes in governmental or political roles.

Fictional presentations in the media attribute evil and suffering to personal, not social or political . . . problems presented, thus distracting attention from the gains to be achieved through political participation.

Emphasis upon citizen duty in the media (to the extent that it is emphasized) serves to bring the widely recognized but private "do-nothing morality" closer to the official morality of the democratic dogma.

The tendency of media owners, advertisers, and segments of the media audiences to dislike references to the roots of social conflict (class or ethnic) weakens the resonance of the media with the problems of the time and, hence, weakens the power to stimulate political response.

On balance, however, exposure to the media is associated with: (a) interest in politics, (b) higher turnout, (c) joining community organizations, (d) superior information, (e) stronger views, (f) closeness to the party position, (g) strong candidate preferences.[6]

In summary, the mass media — of which newspapers, magazines, television, and radio are politically the most important (probably in that order) — are not highly politicized, generally, and are not expected to be by their users. There are, however, differences in the self-images of the media, and in the expectations of media performance held by citizens of various levels of political interest and activity. Finally, most Americans feel obliged by cultural factors to "keep up with things," and this bedrock of demand for political news and views is satisfied mainly by TV and newspapers – with TV the most popular and most trusted source for the impressions and snippets of knowledge that pass for "keeping up" with public events.

TELEVISION AND RADIO
IN THE OPINION-POLICY PROCESS

In recent years, television and radio have been about as good, in variety and coverage of public service programming, as the economics of the industry and the tastes of the audiences will bear.

Nevertheless, there are matters of special responsibility for the electronic media, if they wish further to improve their ways and to maximize their contribution to the American polity. Some of this special responsibility has to do with the everyday procedures and standard operational rules of the networks and stations: Primarily, the tendency toward sponsor and advertising agency pressure on the *political* content of programming should be at all times resisted, as should the tendency toward network domination of individual stations.

Pressures toward conformity and the avoidance of controversy continue to be reported – like the 1973 sponsors' boycott of the CBS program *Maude*. One may assume that the reported instances of network, sponsor, or advertising agency pressures are only a small fraction of those that go unreported. Pressure from the networks or stations on individual commentators or actors are reported frequently, and scripts are changed. Sometimes programs are "killed" outright. The hardiest and most independent commentators sometimes resign – occasionally with fanfare and drama – rather than suffer the subtle censorship, or the threat of censorship, that is in Eric Sevareid's words like "being bitten to death by ducks."

Resisting the tendencies to provincialism, timidity, and economic selfishness, whether these tendencies have their origin in networks, sponsors, or advertising agencies, is only the negative side of the political responsibilities of the electronic mass media. Equally important are the positive obligations of communications channels: primarily, to continue to provide ready opportunities for minority points of view – and, to put the matter most plainly, this does not mean the reluctant airing of less popular views only when FCC rules seem to demand it, but the constant searching out of important issues and the encouragement of integrity and conviction by owners, managers, producers, and commentators. Similarly, advertisers are obliged to support public service programs, recognizing that sponsorship does not commit the advertisers and their regional business outlets to the endorsement of the views expressed on the program.

During political campaigns the electronic media, and especially television, have additional obligations.[7] The importance of television and radio in modern campaigning is attested both by the numbers of citizens who can be (and sometimes are) reached by political programs and by the large proportion of campaign budgets devoted to television and radio coverage. In 1960 an estimated 115,000,000 persons watched one or more of the presidential "Great Debates." These pioneering confrontations of presidential candidates before a national television audience – however good or bad they may have been, and however important for the outcome of the election – were only the first of hundreds of smaller debates in 1960, and each general election since, between senatorial, gubernatorial, congressional, and even city and county candidates. For such joint appearances (which are sometimes made at station or network expense) and for thousands of more traditional campaign programs, not to mention tens of thousands of film clips and spot announcements, candidates for the highest state and national offices will spend, typically, a third to a half or more of their campaign budgets.

It was estimated that all candidates for public office spent a total of $59.6 million on radio and television in 1972. The Federal Election Campaign Act of 1971 made some changes that render impossible comparisons of 1972 and earlier spending. The Act limits media spending by candidates for federal office to ten cents multiplied by the voting age population of their district, or $50,000, whichever is greater; and not more than 60 percent of that total may be spent on television and radio. Presidential candidates spent a total of $10.5 million in the 1972 general election (down from $18.7 million in 1968); Senate candidates spent $6.4 million in 1972, compared with $10.4 million in 1968;

House spending on TV and radio was up, from $6.1 million in 1970 to $7.4 million in 1972.[8]

After the 1968 election Herbert Alexander, Director of the Citizens Research Foundation and the nation's leading expert on campaign financing, estimated that overall spending in presidential campaigns increases about 20 percent every four years. Because of the 1971 Act that may no longer be true, but on cost-of-living grounds alone campaigning expenses are almost certain to continue to rise.[9]

In the national regulation of political television and radio two doctrines are of central importance: the fairness rule and the equal time rule.

The Fairness Doctrine

In 1949 the Federal Communication Commission authorized editorializing by radio and television stations. The Commission at that time established two general requirements of stations: That they (1) "devote a reasonable portion of broadcast time to the discussion and consideration of controversial issues of public importance. . . . [and they] make the facilities available for the expression of contrasting viewpoints when controversial issues are presented."[10] In the application of these general requirements station managers were to exercise their "best judgment and good sense."

But we know that lawyers and bureaucrats are uneasy with phrases like "best judgment and good sense." We also know that air time is a most valuable economic and political commodity. It should not surprise us to learn that station managers, advertisers, and political candidates all sought greater specificity in the application of the fairness doctrine.

In response to such desires the FCC held a comprehensive review — five days of panels and hearings — in 1972. The Commission, to its credit, refused to make detailed regulations or guidelines for what constitutes fairness. It said that the "genius" of the fairness doctrine lay in the leeway it allowed station managers to contribute to an informed electorate, and that more detailed Commission regulations might inhibit those contributions. The Commission continues to referee the matter by taking cases about the application of the doctrine in specific circumstances. Through that process the Commission and its staff have in recent years provided some direction, case by case, with regard to:

1. Editorial advertising, that is, *selling* time to people who want to support or oppose a public policy. The rule seems to be that a station cannot flatly refuse to take such advertising, but presumably libelous or unreasonable editorial advertising could be refused.

2. Countercommercials, that is, free public service announcements specifically pointing out the dangers or deceptiveness of commercially advertised products (example: the American Cancer Society's antismoking ads). The Commission is reluctant to require station managers to take countercommercials. In a case about allegedly fraudulent toy ads, the Commission said the fairness doctrine should not be applied to claims regarding the "efficacy or social utility" of general product advertising.

3. Response time, that is, free opportunity for reply by groups that claim they have been damaged by programs broadcast. The generalization here is that stations must provide time for rebuttals by organizations that have some representative quality, but single individuals do not necessarily have the right to request response time. Response time is appropriate only in the case of "controversial issues" — a matter of interpretation. Judicial reform, for example, appears to be a controversial issue to the FCC, while military recruiting is not.

4. Personal attack. An individual specifically singled out for criticism by a station must be so notified, furnished with a script or tape of the criticism, and given a reasonable and timely opportunity to respond.

Equal Time

Section 315 of the Communications Act requires that when free air time is offered to one candidate, then all the other candidates for that office must be offered equal time. The Commission and the courts have consistently applied this requirement in spirit and letter — with consequences that would be merely ludicrous were they not damaging to the political process. If every minor and publicity-seeking candidate must be offered time equal to that given major candidates the result, predictably, is that TV and radio stations will offer no one free time.

There is one general exception to the equal time requirement. When a bona fide news program carries a report or film clip of, or a brief statement by, a candidate, then other candidates do not have to be given precisely equal time or treatment. As would be expected, much of the controversy about the application of the equal time rules comes on the point of what is and what is not a "bona fide news program." The national and local news summaries aired at the dinner hour and again at 11 P.M. are clearly "bona fide" and exempt from equal time. Recent rulings by the Commission seem to make almost any other kind of candidate appearance subject to equal time provisions. Consequently, networks are reluctant to present the major candidates on question-and-answer shows (like *Meet the Press, Face the Nation,* and their locally aired imitations), because to do so requires expensive equal commitments to minor and nuisance candidates.

For the last twenty years every study of campaign financing and regulation has recommended revision or abolition of the equal time provision. In a spurt of experimental energy Congress exempted the 1960 presidential race from the equal time requirement, but it has not done even that in the last three presidential campaigns. There are two main reasons why the equal time provision is not amended or abolished. One is that incumbents who are running for re-election are advantaged by the rule. As incumbents they get more exposure on bona fide news programs, and they are usually better known generally than their major opponents. They need public service, that is, free, television and radio time less than their major challengers do. And since incumbent members of Congress are the very ones who would have to revise a rule that benefits them, it must be clear why revisions have not yet been made.

The second reason for the failure, so far, to amend the equal time provision of Section 315 is that there are, indeed, serious questions of fairness to all candidates who might be affected. Should TV and radio managers be given complete freedom to select some candidates for free time and ignore other candidates for the same office? Should the law give free time only to the Democratic and Republican parties' candidates? Or should the FCC itself be authorized to choose in each race, each election year, which candidates are major enough to receive free time and which are not?

Some Suggestions for Free and Reduced-Rate Time

Speculation on these questions seems to end in general agreement that the law should require some substantial free time for major candidates (say, a total of three or four hours of network time for a presidential candidate), with proportionately less for other candidates who qualify for the same office. Thus in a United States Senate race, for example, the Democratic and Republican parties' candidates might be given one prime-time hour each (not necessarily all at once), and the candidates of the other parties fifteen minutes each. Such formulas for allocation of free time would rest on the presumption that candidates who have no popular support would not be on the ballot (since the state laws ordinarily require voters' signatures for a person to qualify as a minor or third-party candidate). Allocations should give exposure to the more important races and candidates without requiring the media to spend more resources than they can justify, or more time than their audiences want, on marginal and often quite irrelevant candidacies.[11] The British for years have allocated free campaign broadcast time proportionately on the basis of votes obtained by the various parties. Such allocations would be more complex in America, but not unworkable.

The television and radio industries, networks, and individual stations alike should be expected (and required by the FCC, if necessary) to provide additional special opportunities for candidates during campaigns. To avoid hardship to the television and radio broadcasters, and to keep within the tolerance level of the apolitical portion of mass audiences, free or reduced-rate political time should be limited to a short period (say, thirty days) before the election. The current practice is for some free TV and radio time to be given to candidates, either directly or through the airing of bipartisan panels and forums sponsored by citizenship groups like the League of Women Voters. Little such free time is available, however.

A guaranteed minimum amount of free time, or combination of free and reduced-rate time, should be made available in a general election to all candidates running in a constituency that is greater than some minimum geographical size. For example, the law (or FCC ruling) might say that TV or radio stations must give thirty minutes of free time to each general-election candidate in all constituencies that equal half or more of the broadcast area. To limit the free-time period to general elections would avoid the intricacies of defining candidacy and the burden of providing time for large numbers of primary aspirants in some areas; it would also have the salutary effect of encouraging the minority party to field candidates, and thus speed the development of two-partyism generally.

In addition to free time for the major, general-election candidates, reduced-rate time might be required for other candidates within the broadcast area. It is not desirable, of course, that *all* candidates be given reduced-rate time; a sound policy would be to discourage, rather than encourage, political broadcasts over a large area of which only a small fraction is in the constituency of the candidate. The citizens of twenty-four wards of a city should not be required to suffer the compulsory loss of a TV channel so that the councilmanic candidate of the twenty-fifth ward can appeal to one-twenty-fifth of the potential viewers. Obviously, any requirement of free or reduced-rate time must be sensible in its coverage and applied with good judgment.

Besides the provision for free campaigning time, television and radio stations ought to take positions on issues and candidates. Since 1949 individual stations have been free to editorialize, but few have taken advantage of the opportunity. Indeed, it was not until October 27, 1960, that an American radio station endorsed a candidate for president of the United States. On that evening, at 10:35 P.M., WMCA, New York, declared itself for John F. Kennedy, and declared that it would take its "public responsibility seriously, even when it means running risks of being ahead of the times." That WMCA was ahead of the times is not to be doubted, for less than one-third of American television and radio stations seem to be editorializing at all, and only a very few support candidates by name. There is, as yet, no evidence that the stations that editorialize have been harmed by the practice.

Campaigning and Television Confrontations

Television is clearly of great importance as a campaigning medium. Joint appearances and other dramatic devices have become common campaign features of the major races — and have lost some impact by becoming common. In 1962 Angus Campbell, of the University of Michigan's Survey Research Center, summarized TV's impact on campaigning as follows:

[*It*] has succeeded in making a sizable part of the electorate direct witnesses to episodes in recent political history. . . . It has greatly extended the purely visual dimension of political communication; the public no doubt finds it easier to form an image of its political leaders. . . . But it seems neither to have elevated the general level of political interest nor to have broadened the total range of political information. . . . people who follow the election campaigns most closely on television are precisely the same ones who read about them in the newspapers and magazines. . . . Rather than adding an important new dimension to the total flow of information to the public, [television] seems largely to have taken over the role of radio.[12]

Campbell's view in 1962 was that TV has not generally changed the nature of political campaigns in America. That conclusion has been disputed. Some research by Philip Converse, also published in 1962, suggested that the party loyalty of apolitical Americans is weakened when they are exposed to new political stimuli on TV (or any other medium), but for people already interested in politics new TV information is irrelevant to, or may actually strengthen, party loyalty.[13] Dreyer's 1971 research, updating Converse's work, did not find that less informed and less motivated Americans were more influenced by media exposure than were politically active persons.[14] It is therefore not clear that television has special influence on the political attitudes of our least interested citizens — though I think it is probable that it does, since we know they are most likely to get political cues from TV (if they get any at all) and that they have fewer competing sources of cues. Thus TV campaigning probably does make a difference in the most visible and important races.

In an insightful speculative article, Wamsley and Pride have recently argued that TV *news* broadcasts may have profound, pervasive, and long-term impact on the attitudes and behaviors of Americans. TV news, they argue, injects a continuous flow of potent symbols into the political environment. Viewers get political cues without seeking them, and from a trusted source; *perceptions* of the world are changed, and changed perceptions often bring about attitude change later. And even if mass attitudes do not change, or change ever so slowly, do not repeated TV news emphases allow political elites more scope for change? "How much sooner," these scholars ask, "did a large segment of the political elite shift to a position against the Vietnam war because of TV news reports? . . . And how much more rapidly have ecological efforts snowballed and the issue become popular with both parties because of TV coverage of the subject? Perhaps these questions cannot be answered in the current state of social science, but more likely we have not devoted sufficient ingenuity to the quest."[15]

THE PRESS AND THE OPINION-POLICY PROCESS

The short history of American newspapers is that of eighteenth-century publications that depended on politics, and how they became twentieth-century publications upon which politics depends. This statement, like all epigrams, exaggerates its message: Newspapers were never wholly political; and only in a few places in this century can it be said that politics depends on newspaper influence. Yet the general historical change in American newspapers is clear: They were once thoroughly political; but their political interests are now apt to be vague, occasional, and of no great importance to their own economic life. Although newspapers remain the most consciously political of the mass media — reflecting both their traditions and the expectations of their readers — the pervasiveness of politics, characteristic of early newspapers, has generally given way both to moderation in tone and to a physical separation of news from political advice (that is, from *editorializing*).

Most American newspapers are still political to the extent that in editorials, and occasionally in their selection of news to report, they may support or attack public figures and public policies. But the age of moderation, gentility, and the soft sell has come to newspapers, and only rarely does one encounter highly emotional or *ad hominem* political journalism — except for a few syndicated columns written by men whose stock-in-trade is extremism.

There are many differences between the older style of political journalism, as practiced by Greeley, Dana, Pulitzer, and Hearst in the nineteenth century, and modern political journalism. The political journalism of the last century was personal; in this century, it is institutional. Editorial pages are increasingly the products of groups of men, editors and managers, who do not make the policy of the paper.

It should not be thought that the large American newspapers are worse for their change from personalism to institutionalism. They are unquestionably better in their service to the balance, judiciousness, and moderation that, in any well-ordered society, must be central to the opinion-policy process. Not only are editorials of the major newspapers joint endeavors, which, like all products of committees, must respect the law of the lowest common denominator, but what passion remains is syndicated, nationalized, and mailed-in. Thus, William Buckley writes his national column from the New York office of his national magazine; and Jack Anderson writes his political gossip from Washington. Their indignation is inevitably muffled by the time lag between the writing and the reading in a hundred local dailies and by the requirement that a national audience must be fed commentary on national (and thus, for most people, less interesting) events.

Sheer size, too, has contributed to the increase of blandness on the editorial pages of our newspapers. A mass-circulation paper cannot support extreme political journalism — the modal newspaper reader is not an extremist. A highly partisan paper may please those who are highly partisan; but such readers are too few to support large papers. When the 125-year-old *Boston Herald-Traveler* folded in the spring of 1972 it sold its "name, good will, and physical assets" to the Hearst chain's *Record-American*. The *Herald-Traveler*, it was said, had been "for decades the voice of Boston's Republican establishment."[16] To keep those old *Herald-Traveler* readers the *Record-American* must, to some extent, absorb also the politics of the defunct paper. Thus mass circulation begets accommodation and moderation.

Finally, the politics of moderation has a clear benefit not found in the extremely partisan papers of earlier times. Moderate papers will air controversy and opposing views within the limits of the moderate middle. The *Los Angeles Times* recently drew attention to these evolving characteristics of big papers.

> By the turn of the century a more comprehensive paper was emerging. It sought a wider audience than the audience afforded by party or faction. . . . This trend toward the comprehensive newspaper has continued to the present day. . . .With the development toward fewer and larger metropolitan newspapers came both a decline in partisanship and an increased effort by newspapers to look behind the daily flow of surface events to examine their causes and consequences. This attempt to put events into context is more useful to the readers than a mere account of daily events — in fact it is essential — but it is also much more difficult to do well. It requires professionalism and good judgment and above all a sense of fairness.[17]

Biases of the American Press

American newspapers are generally conservative, jealous of their independence from governmental regulation, and presumptuous, but probably they are our most important safeguard against the manifold evils to which any large public might fall prey.

The characteristic biases of the American press are all displayed at the annual meetings of the American Newspaper Publishers Association. In April of each year that group meets to review and report itself. Its committees invariably denounce governments for overzealous regulation of the media, for favoring unions in labor-management disputes, for "indiscriminate subpoenas of professional newsmen" (1972), and, as recently as 1960, for regulating child labor, because "the training of a newspaper boy was one of the country's strongest deterrents to juvenile delinquency." Taxes on advertising and on circulation are especially noxious to the A.N.P.A., as are any attempts by the Postal Service to raise the second-class mail rates, which have for decades subsidized the newspaper industry. The A.N.P.A. continues its practice of "accrediting" journalism schools and departments; about 50 schools have been blessed with the seal of approval of this self-interested private group.

The presumptuousness especially of newspapers hardly needs to be documented — it is apparent at all times. The usual American newspaper coverage of prisoners charged with lurid crimes is so prejudicial to their rights of due process of law as to be unacceptable to even the most minimal standards of fair play — and to be illegal in countries that follow the British practice. A central part is played by the press in the public condemnations, prejudgments, vilifications and horror (real and pretended) of alleged murderers and rapists. Celebrated recent cases of journalistic judging include those of Lee Harvey Oswald, the alleged assassin of President Kennedy, who was exterminated by a media-inflamed citizen; of mass murderer Juan Corona in 1971; and of the seemingly endless publicity on the Watergate indictments that began in 1972.

That American newspapers have a high and exaggerated notion of their own importance is beyond doubt. But it is also beyond doubt that newspapers are important, indeed, indispensable elements in the public discussion and criticism that is fundamental to self-government. The foregoing critical comments do not mean that journalists should have any lesser view of their responsibilities and their importance, but only that they should be ever aware of the fallibility of their judgments, and of those tendencies (which they share with all of us) to mistake their own interests for the general interest. Precisely because they are so important in the opinion-policy process, newspapers should strive for *extraordinary* humility.

The biases of the American press have historic, economic, and political roots. The best newspapermen are acutely aware of the deep tradition of free inquiry in Western civilization and of the importance of printing in the history of intellectual controversy. And the most able present-day American newspapermen have a deep commitment to the arguments of Milton's *Areopagitica* and a deep sense of participation in the honored profession of Peter Zenger and William Lloyd Garrison.

Sometimes freedom of the press means having the guts to resist intimidation and imprisonment, as did William Near, whose outspoken attacks on public officials led to the Supreme Court's determination that the national government would guarantee newspapers against censorship by state and local authorities (*Near* v. *Minnesota*, 283 U.S. 697, 1931).

Sometimes freedom of the press means great confrontations by major institutions of our society — as when the *New York Times* resisted the Senate committee's claim to wholesale investigation of its employees (*New York Times*, January 5, 1956), when it published *The Pentagon Papers*, defying the Nixon administration's claim that "national security" (as it alone defined that term) took precedence over the First Amendment (*New York Times Co.* v. *U.S.*, 403 U.S. 713, 1971).

Sometimes freedom of the press is asserted more informally, with a light touch — as when Georgia's Governor Lester Maddox called the editors of the *Atlanta Constitution* "lying devils and dirty dogs" and threatened personally to picket their offices. The *Constitution* on that occasion editorially reminded their readers that they had been picketed by the Ku Klux Klan, antifluoridationists, women's libbers, and the Committee to Stamp Out the Fire Ant. "Newspapers," they said, "like people, can be measured by the enemies they make. We are proud of ours. So welcome, Governor. . . . You won't bother us. We are used to characters carrying signs."[18]

It used to be thought that the conservative bias of the American press was maintained by a small and selfish group of wealthy investors and capitalists who prevented liberal reporters and "the common people" from expressing liberal or radical sentiments. Nowadays, the conservative bias of the American newspapers is usually attributed to more subtle factors, related to the nature of the industry. A major daily newspaper is a large business enterprise, having most of the characteristics of all large business enterprises. It usually has a corporate form, a large and expensive plant, and a management separated from its ownership —

although it is still not uncommon for newspapers to retain a "family-corporate" flavor, like those of the Hearst, Chandler, Cox, and Cowles interests. It is enough to explain in large part why newspapers unheroically support the status quo to observe that while newspapers may have been "started by men who had something to say, they are carried on by men who have something to sell."[19]

The major antidotes to bias and falsification in newspapers are (a) economic competition and (b) governmental regulation. Of these two, governmental regulation is the less favored in America; it has been resorted to only in the more flagrant cases, such as libel and grossly misleading, subversive, or inflammatory publication.

As an inhibitor of press bias, economic competition is, first, a matter of alternative sources of news and opinions for the citizenry, and, second, a matter of what the employees of the paper and its readers will tolerate. It goes almost without saying that monopoly control of the dissemination of news and opinions gives the monopolist an opportunity for unlimited bias and distortion of truth. The rulers of a totalitarian society, by definition, have such a monopoly; but it seems unlikely that such control has ever existed in the United States — even in the smallest and most isolated company-owned mining town in the West.

In the United States today, many sources of news and opinion exist. Although there are fewer daily newspapers now than there were in 1900, there are important alternative news sources that did not exist in 1900. In recent years, much has been made of the fact that, through bankruptcy and mergers, many newspapers have closed in the past four or five decades, with a consequence that there are many one-newspaper cities. In 1915 there were 2,502 daily newspapers in America; and in 1973 there were 1,764. Since the middle 1950s the number of dailies has remained nearly constant. Because of the earlier rapid decrease in the number of papers through bankruptcies and mergers, it is often said that the monopolies enjoyed in one-newspaper towns encourage or at least increase the likelihood of distortion, slanting the news, irresponsible exercise of editorial power, and the like.

The further claim is made that monopoly newspapers often get a large share of their stories from monopoly news-gathering agencies — one or the other of the two great "wire services" in America. Thus the argument is that the wire services may distort or selectively report the news, and such distorted and selectively reported news may be further distorted or biased by local judgment of what to print. Monopoly, it is charged, shows its ugly power in the news-gathering agency when only one is subscribed to, and at the local editor's desk in one-newspaper communities. What little evidence is available indicates that one-wire-service small dailies do in fact print a pattern of categories of stories much like one another and much like that sent to them on the wire service "ticker." It is unclear whether the critical judgment of local editors just happens to coincide with the critical judgment of wire-service editors on what kinds of news to disseminate or, as seems more probable to me, that the wire-service judgments are uncritically accepted by editors of small-town dailies.[20] Charges of bias in one-newspaper towns are heard most often from liberals and reformers, because it is they who feel most consciously the general conservatism of American newspapers.

An imaginative study of two similar middle-sized urban areas — one with a media monopoly and the other with a competitive media pattern — was conducted during 1970. Representative samples of adults in York, Pennsylvania (pop. 101,000), and Zanesville, Ohio (pop. 82,000), were interviewed twice, in April and in June. An elite panel was also drawn for York. The contrast in media patterns was remarkable. In 1970 York was the only city of its size with all newspaper and broadcast media under separate and economically unrelated ownership; there were two daily papers, two TV stations, and six AM or FM radio outlets, all independent of each other. Zanesville, by contrast, was a thorough media monopoly; one newspaper, one TV station, and one radio station, with both AM and FM facilities, all owned and operated by the Zanesville Publishing Company, Mr. Clay Littick, President. On tests of knowledge-ability of places-things-names in the news, York residents scored significantly higher, and this superiority was confirmed in subtests of carefully matched individual respondents. Although the citizens of Zanesville have equal opportunity to get news and opinions from outside their community, the researchers discovered that they are "substantially more dependent upon local media than are the people of York. . . . Thus, those who operate the media in Zanesville are in better position to influence the political and other attitudes of the public than are those who operate the media in York."[21] Local media monopolies, this research seems to demonstrate, are detrimental to the electoral politics of democracies because the lack of an organized dialogue *delays* the crystallization of opinions about national and state candidates, and may even *prevent* the full exposure of information about local candidates. "There is," this report concludes, "no question but that a media monopoly does have an adverse influence on the knowledgeability and political flexibility of the local audiences it serves."[22]

In sum, the general social and political biases of American newspapers are what one would expect, given the large-business and corporate perspectives of their policy makers, the imperatives of competition for recency and sensation – for the titillation of audiences that consist mainly of persons uninterested in public issues – and the endemic lack of journalistic talent to write and edit their millions of daily lines.

Newspapers and Partisanship

As one would also expect, in view of the conservatism of the American press, most newspapers support Republican Party policies and Republican candidates. At least such is the big generalization – which, like most big generalizations, does not take us far on the road to understanding. The pro-Republican tendencies of American newspapers are by no means simple or direct; we must have some information on three subtopics in order to appreciate more clearly whether, or to what extent, a pro-Republican bias in newspapers is a matter of importance to the opinion-policy process. We need to know (a) how self-consciously pro-Republican American papers are (that is, how many newspapers intend to be pro-Republican in their editorial policy); (b) how the biases are shown generally and at critical junctures in the governing process (e.g., in election campaigns and votes on public issues); and (c) how newspaper favoritism affects the outcome of electoral decisions.

Most newspapers adopt an official stance of nonpartisanship or political independence. The rhetoric of the free press places a high value on the word *independence*. Because of differences in sample size and bases of reporting, the rate of change to a nominal independency may be exaggerated in Table 6-1, but the long-run trend is quite clearly away from partisan self-identification.

Another index of how partisan newspapers intend to be is their record of endorsements for public office. Because the only national election in the United States is that for president, the quadrennial scorecards of newspaper support for major-party candidates will give us some idea of the preponderance of Republicanism among American papers.

TABLE 6-1.   The Self-Reported Partisanship of Daily Newspapers
in America, 1944, 1960, and 1972*

	1944		1960		1972	
	N	%	N	N	N	%
Independent	845	47.9	213	61.0	285	68.3
Independent-Republican and Republican	470	26.6	68	19.5	68	16.3
Independent-Democratic and Democratic	451	25.5	68	19.5	64	15.3
Total	1,766	100.0	349	100.0	417	99.9

*Data from Frank Luther Mott. "Newspapers in Presidential Campaigns," *Public Opinion Quarterly*, VIII (1944), 366, and *The Working Press of the Nation* (Chicago: The National Research Bureau), the 1960 and 1972 editions.

In 1956 slightly over half of the dailies in the country endorsed one of the major-party candidates; 740 (80 percent) supported Republican President Eisenhower and 189 (20 percent) backed Democrat Adlai Stevenson. In 1960, of the papers endorsing a presidential candidate, 731 (78 percent) backed Republican Richard M. Nixon and 208 (22 percent) endorsed Democrat John F. Kennedy. In 1964, using the same measurement, 349 (45 percent) supported Republican Barry Goldwater and 440 (55 percent) supported Democrat Lyndon B. Johnson. In 1968, 792 papers endorsed a presidential candidate: 634 (80.1 percent) supported Republican Richard M. Nixon; 146 (18.4 percent), Democrat Hubert H. Humphrey; and 12 (1.5 percent), third-party candidate George C. Wallace. In 1972, 753 papers (93 percent) supported President Nixon for re-election and 56 (7 percent) supported Democrat George McGovern.[23]

In the 1970s there may be a tendency for newspapers to de-emphasize the endorsement of partisan candidates. The Newark (New Jersey) *Star-Ledger* announced in 1973 that it would no longer endorse any candidates: *Newsday*, a relatively new but highly regarded daily on Long Island, adopted the same policy in 1972; and the *Los Angeles Times* in 1973 decided to end endorsements in presidential, gubernatorial, and United States Senate races.

Very little study has been made of newspaper endorsements of state and local candidates. It is probably safe to assume that papers endorse more Republicans than Democrats, judging from the distribution of presidential-candidate endorsements and from the findings of the few state and local studies. In one analysis of statewide campaigns in Connecticut and Wisconsin, of the eleven dailies chosen in Wisconsin four supported the Republican candidates, two supported the Democratic, and four were neutral; in Connecticut no one of the nine dailies supported the Democrats — but the authors unfortunately do not indicate how many of the nine papers were pro-Republican and how many were neutral.[24] In another study of newspaper treatment of partisan candidates and campaigning, this one in Pennsylvania, of twenty-six papers nine endorsed the two Republican candidates (for governor and United States senator), three supported the two Democrats, four divided their endorsements, and ten papers remained neutral.[25]

In a careful study of editorial endorsements in California newspapers, James E. Gregg found that "80 percent are Republican in orientation, 10 percent are Democratic in orientation and 10 percent are either truly independent or are papers which do not make political endorsements."[26] Gregg suggests that it is a "sham" for 75 percent of California's newspapers to have claimed (in 1963) they were politically independent.

Aside from self-admitted partisanship, and from the endorsement of partisan candidates, is there evidence that American newspapers show partisan favoritism in their treatment of news? If the newspapers have a genuinely conservative bias as a result of their owners' and managers' general identification with big business, might they not expose this bias in giving preferential treatment to conservative candidates generally and especially to Republican candidates? To argue that this is likely to be the case is not necessarily to ascribe conscious favoritism to the newspaper managers (though conscious favoritism is consistent with at least one tradition of American journalism); such favoritism might result from an accumulation of small advantages of news slanting or selection or placement in favor of the approved candidates. For information bearing on intended and unintended bias we must turn to content analyses of newspapers during campaigns. The author of one national study of thirty-five daily papers concluded that

> there was slanting in the news columns during the 1952 election, but it was not as widespread as some critics have maintained. A majority of the newspapers in this study — eighteen — met the highest standards of fair news presentation, and a large number of newspapers — eleven — showed no significant degree of partiality that would warrant a charge of unfairness. The six newspapers found to have demonstrated partiality in their news columns constitute a minority.

It also is evident that newspapers which supported the Republican presidential candidate performed, on the whole, at a higher level than did the pro-Democratic newspapers.[27]

Studies of fifteen major American dailies' treatment of the 1960 and 1964 presidential campaigns concluded that there was such good balance and equal coverage, quantitatively, that there must have been conscious efforts on the part of editors for a 50-50 treatment.[28] However, an analysis of the prestige press in 1968 showed systematic bias. On five dimensions of coverage — news articles, opinion articles, pictures, headlines, and letters to the editor — ten prestige dailies "demonstrated favorable treatments corresponding to their editorial endorsements in major items of all main categories of their campaign coverage."[29]

Finally, an imaginative comparison of newspaper treatments of the 1896 and 1952 presidential campaigns found a great difference between the partisan favoritism and distortion in the 1896 campaign and the much more nearly fair and equal treatment given the candidates in the 1952 campaign.[30]

To this point, our look at the partisanship of American newspapers reveals that most papers describe themselves as independent, and that of those admitting a partisan preference, the Democratic-Republican split is about even. However, as measured by endorsement of partisan candidates, the newspapers as a whole seem significantly Republican, by 60 to 80 percent of the endorsements made in national, state, and local elections. Measurements of partisan bias in newspapers indicate that, overall, Republicans get more favorable treatment than do Democrats; but this finding seems to be significantly less true of the larger and more influential dailies. On the whole, the claims of some Democrats that America has a "one-party press" seem greatly exaggerated, although based on a kernel of truth.

Another different but at least equally important question is whether partisan favoritism by newspapers actually helps the favored candidate. Here again most of our knowledge is about presidential elections. The best historical study, reviewing two-party presidential campaigns since 1800, reported no evidence that newspapers unduly affect presidential races.[31]

But Mott's generalization refers only to presidential campaigns, which are so visible and played on by so many forces that one is not surprised to find no demonstrably great influence from newspaper endorsement.[32] What of the thousands of more obscure state and local candidacies, often run in jurisdictions where only a few communications channels exist — are newspapers, under such circumstances, not more influential for election outcomes? The answer seems to be "yes," although the evidence is too scanty to be conclusive. In the study of Wisconsin and Connecticut statewide races mentioned earlier, all three candidates favored by the majority of the newspapers won their races; but the Pennsylvania study of 1958, for a variety of reasons, is inconclusive on the point.

Gregg's examination of California papers from 1948 through 1962 reveals that endorsements for local officers are more efficacious than for state or national office. Eleven papers with 40 percent of total state circulation, in the fourteen years of candidate endorsements, had an average of 84.1 percent winners in local elections, compared with averages of 63.6 to 73.8 percent for a variety of district-wide and state-wide elections. Gregg also found, as he hypothesized, that newspaper endorsements for referendum measures were even more effective than endorsements for candidates.[33]

A striking example of the importance of newspaper endorsements occurred in the 1969 Los Angeles County race for seven nonpartisan seats in a newly created junior college district. One hundred thirty-three candidates filed, with no one having the advantage of incumbency or party support. In that bewildering situation voters apparently turned to newspaper endorsements as cues for voting. An analysis of the results showed that *Los Angeles Times*-endorsed candidates got "an extra 24,000 votes and the *Herald-Examiner* candidates gained some 9,000."[34]

Finally, there is some survey research evidence that readers' overall perceptions of how their daily newspaper leans in an election (perceptions gained from editorials, news, and other cues) will influence them in the same direction. From the Michigan Survey Research Center's 1968 data, Robinson concludes that, "with other variables controlled, it was estimated that a newspaper's perceived support of one candidate rather than another was associated with about a 6 percent edge in vote for the endorsed candidate over his opponent."[35] Perhaps 6 percent of the readers (or an even larger minority) are able to find cues for voting in their paper. But most, apparently, do not. Doris Graber investigated the images held by American voters about the presidential candidates in 1968. At the same time she reviewed the contents of 20 major national and regional newspapers to see what images of the candidates they were publishing. Her findings confirmed that "the stress on personal image qualities . . . of the average American is, indeed, paralleled by a heavy emphasis on personal qualities in the press." But the press also laid before its readers a vast amount of information about the candidates — most of which was neutral and offered few evaluative clues (the newspapers' biases, in her judgment, were restricted mainly to editorials). She concludes that in the "torrent" of information "people may have settled for the easy solution of ignoring all but the most readily absorbed human traits, or relying largely on party labels."[36]

THE PRESS, GOVERNMENT, AND THE FREE SOCIETY

There is an inevitable symbiosis between public policymakers and the press. Cohen describes it in systems terminology:

The mechanism involved here is a feedback loop, in the sense that foreign policy officials dominate the public discussion of a policy, which they (and Congressmen also) then monitor and on the basis of which they draw conclusions about their freedom to take the next steps. The loop may not even go any further or deeper than the media of communication; the public relations activity results in press coverage, which is then interpreted as significant public opinion.[37]

Thus "public opinion" on foreign policies often becomes the jelling of the views of officials and media opinion leaders, and few if any other individuals or groups are part of the process. No doubt the evolution of domestic policies involves wider participation, but this symbiosis of officialdom and media (especially the press) is a constant factor in decisionmaking, and fundamental to the media's importance.

Modern journalism suffers from the stultifying conventions that have to do with "newspaper style" and the demand for immediacy. The archaic rules of newspaper style require that a "good story" tell only what happened since the last issue of the paper and that the essential features of the story be summarized in a few crisp sentences in the very first paragraph. This requirement, of course, is absurd. Most of the important news of any day is not new at all, but a development of yesterday's news, as that news was a development of the news of the day before. The pretense that public events are discontinuous not merely distorts the facts but exaggerates the ordinary citizen's tendency to envision the impersonal world of public affairs as episodic snippets of reality rather than as a flow of interrelated events. The best news media strive to place the events of the day in perspective, but there is still entirely too much effort to isolate, concentrate, and capsulate the news into "flashes."

Paletz and his collaborators suggest that the professional conventions of journalism produce stories that are uncritically supportive of local government officials. They investigated the activities of the Durham, North Carolina, city council and the way those activities were reported in the only paper that regularly covered the council. They concluded that ". . . the media do not increase and may diminish public interest in institutions and individuals vested with local authority... by not covering those who hold such authority, or by reporting their activities in ways supportive of their authority. One result is often to insulate city councils from informed public scrutiny."[38]

That long embarrassment called Watergate provided an historic set of examples of what is best and worst in American investigative reporting. For five months after the burglarizing of the Democratic National Committee Headquarters the papers reported the event almost as though it were an ordinary story of crime in a big city. Senator George McGovern, Democratic candidate, tried to make it a major campaign issue, but failed. The inability or the unwillingness of the press to see Watergate as symbolic of thorough corruption in the Republican presidential campaign may have been related to the fact, noted above, that only 7 percent of endorsing dailies were for McGovern. More probably it reflected the preoccupation of the press with day-to-day superficiality and the refusal of most papers and chains to commit their reporters to the slow digging out and piecing together that exposing public conspiracies requires.

George Seldes observed that, although Watergate reporting was later said to be "the finest hour in investigative journalism," the exposure of what he termed "the greatest corruption in American history" was in fact the work of only four of the 1,764 daily papers in the nation – *The Washington Post, The Washington Star-News, The New York Times,* and the *Los Angeles Times* (the last being especially praiseworthy, since it had endorsed Nixon). Seldes pointed out that "the great press chains notoriously failed, or refused, to investigate: Newhouse (21 Washington correspondents, none on Watergate), Copley chain (7 correspondents, none on Watergate). . . . ABC-TV and Radio, with 16 correspondents, CBS and NBC, each with 25, and not one on Watergate."[39] One hardly knows, looking back through the fog and stench of Watergate, whether to condemn the 1,760 dailies that treated it as usual politics or to applaud those four that saw it for the massive and intolerable shame that it was.

Alert journalists can usually find ways to discover the facts in local, state, and national news. Acting as the agents of "the people's right to know," a role in which they like to cast themselves, they can ordinarily ferret out all the facts that the people need to know about domestic public policy, even when information is withheld by government officials who feel threatened by such exposures. Reporters may not always be able to ferret out the facts from one source, but with the help of officials in other branches or levels of government (congressmen, state legislators, or attorneys general), the energetic press can well perform its responsibilities as critic and scrutinizer of the public's business.[40]

The task of obtaining facts is not so easy, however, with regard to foreign and defense policy. The problems of unfamiliarity, complexity, geographical distance, and espionage (real and imagined) are so great in foreign and military affairs that even a minimum public consideration of national policy in these areas demands the closest cooperation and understanding between governmental officials and the news media. It is not surprising that very often officials and newsmen disagree about where the balance should be struck between secrecy and exposure.

Governmental information policy with respect to sensitive material may range from complete exposure to complete manipulation. The ends of such a continuum are unrealistic, of course, because no nation under present or foreseeable international conditions is prepared to tell all it knows, and no country is totalitarian enough to manipulate *all* information successfully. What is practical, however, even in a nation with strong traditions of an open and free press, is a policy that employs selective openness and closedness with regard to what the media are given by government officials. Public officials, like other human beings, prefer to have their work and their organizations well thought of. When government officials have convinced themselves that the "national interest" requires it, they have withheld from the public some or all of the news about events, or some or all of the explanations about policy. The historic complaint of newsmen (and congressmen) is that the administrative agencies do not tell all they know. In some cases no information may be given about an event or policy; in other cases selectively misleading or inadequate information may be given.

Something more than mere withholding is implied by the notion of governmental "management" of the news. News "management" involves the deliberate creation of partial truths, or of outright falsehoods, in the furtherance of a governmental policy. That "management" is used by Democratic as well as Republican administrations when they feel that the national security interests require it is attested by the bold-faced statements of Assistant Secretary for Defense Arthur Sylvester in October 1962. In the crisis over Soviet missiles in Cuba the United States agencies involved found it expedient to plant several lies in the American press to mislead Cuban and Soviet officials. Sylvester put the matter starkly. "It is inherent in government," he said, "[to have] the right to lie to save itself when going toward a nuclear war. It's basic." The concept Sylvester laid bare is an old one; but he gave it a new name amidst some new frankness: "News as weaponry" means "in the kind of world we live in, [that] the generation of news by actions taken by the government becomes a weapon in a strained situation."[41]

The long history of news manipulation, half lies, and full lies that characterized our Indochina adventures from 1960 to 1972 (and perhaps even yet — who can be sure?) was marked by press connivance in official deception. "Backgrounders" (meetings of reporters and officials that the press agrees to treat anonymously) are a source of much news manipulation. Bill Moyers, former press assistant to President Johnson, believes that backgrounders often become "a primary instrument of policy, propaganda, and manipulation" that "cause harm and create an unbelieving and untrusting public." Sometimes such duplicity gets exposed. But, says Moyer:

In the end very little will change. The Government will go on calling backgrounders as long as the Government wants to put its best face forward. Reporters will be there to report dutifully what isn't officially said by a source that can't be held officially accountable at an event that doesn't officially happen for a public that can't officially be told because it can't officially be trusted to know.[42]

Like all the great abiding tensions that inhere in self-government, the conflict between the demands of secrecy and the right to know must be weighed anew with each decision and within the conscience and good judgment of each decisionmaker. We are committed to the maximum freedom of information; and when there is doubt, this conflict always ought to be resolved in favor of disclosure. A primary responsibility of the mass media, and particularly of the press, is to be what Thomas Jefferson called "the censor of the government."

Notes:

[1] Alfred O. Hero, *Mass Media and World Affairs* (Boston: World Peace Foundation, 1959), p. 110.

[2] For references to earlier studies and for evidence that "involvement with television is associated with a syndrome of conventionality" see Russell H. Weigel and Richard Jessor, "Television and Adolescent Conventionality: An Exploratory Study," *Public Opinion Quarterly*, XXXVII (1973), 76-90. Quote at p. 87.

[3] Maxwell E. McCombs and Donald L. Shaw, "The Agenda-Setting Function of Mass Media," *Public Opinion Quarterly*, XXXVI (1972), 176.

[4] Richard Maisel, "The Decline of Mass Media," *Public Opinion Quarterly*, XXXVII (1973), 159.

[5] See Robert E. Lane, *Political Ideology: Why the Common Man Believes What He Does* (New York: The Free Press, 1962), pp. 373-7.

[6] Robert E. Lane, *Political Life: Why People Get Involved in Politics* (New York: The Free Press, 1959), Chapter 19, "Mass Media and Mass Politics," pp. 275-98; quotation from pp. 288-9. Copyright 1959. Reprinted by permission of The Macmillian Company.

[7] For overviews of television in American politics, see Bernard Rubin, *Political Television* (Belmont, Calif.: Wadsworth Publishing Company, Inc., 1967); Robert MacNeil, *The People Machine* (New York: Harper & Row, Inc., 1968); Sig Mickelson, *The Electric Mirror: Politics in the Age of Television* (New York: Dodd, Mead and Company, 1972); Robert E. Gilbert, *Television and Presidential Politics* (North Quincy, Mass.: The Christopher Publishing House, 1972); and, especially, Marvin Barrett, ed., *The Politics of Broadcasting* (New York: Thomas Y. Crowell Company, 1973) and others of the same series, Columbia University's "Survey of Broadcasting Journalism."

[8] The data in this paragraph are from *Congressional Quarterly*, XXXI, May 12, 1973, 1134-7. For detailed information on financing campaign

and party politics in America, see the many useful publications of The Citizens Research Foundation, 22 Nassau Street, Princeton, New Jersey.

[9] I do not imply that we spend too much on political campaigns. For a persuasive argument that we may spend too little, see David Adamany, *Campaign Finance in America* (North Scituate, Mass.: Duxbury Press, 1972).

[10] Federal Communication Commission, *Thirty-eighth Annual Report; Fiscal Year 1972* (Washington, D.C.: Government Printing Office), p. 32.

[11] In 1972 the FCC ruled that TV comedian Pat Paulsen was subject to the equal time rule because he had filed as a Republican candidate in the New Hampshire primary. The ruling caused some embarrassment for Paulsen's employer, Walt Disney Productions, besides pointing up, again, the absurdity of the present rule.

[12] Angus Campbell, "Has Television Reshaped Politics?" *Columbia Journalism Review*, I (Fall 1962), 13.

[13] Philip E. Converse, "Information Flow and the Stability of Partisan Attitudes," *Public Opinion Quarterly*, XXVI (1962), 578-99.

[14] Edward C. Dreyer, "Media Use and Electoral Choices: Some Political Consequences of Information Exposure," *Public Opinion Quarterly*, XXXV (Winter 1971-72), 544-53.

[15] Gary L. Wamsley and Richard A. Pride, "Television Network News: Rethinking the Iceberg Problem," *Western Political Quarterly*, XXV (September 1972), 434-50, quotation at p. 448. See also Paul H. Weaver, "Is Television News Biased?" *The Public Interest*, No. 26 (Winter 1972), 57-74.

[16] *New York Times*, May 18, 1972.

[17] "Some Changes in the Editorial Pages," *Los Angeles Times*, September 23, 1973.

[18] *Atlanta Constitution*, May 3, 1970.

[19] William L. Rivers, *The Opinion Makers: The Washington Press Corps* (Boston: Beacon Press, 1965), p. 200, quoting Alan Barth.

[20] David Gold and Jerry L. Simmons, "News Selection Patterns Among Iowa Dailies," *Public Opinion Quarterly*, XXIX (1965), 425-30.

[21] *Media Monopoly and Politics* (Washington, D.C.: American Institute for Political Communication, 1973), p. 29.

[22] *Ibid.*, p. 167.

[23] *Editor and Publisher* (November 3, 1956), 11, 64-8; (November 5, 1960), 9-13; (October 31, 1964), 9-13; (November 2, 1968), 9; and (November 4, 1972), 10.

24 LeRoy C. Ferguson and Ralph H. Smuckler, *Politics in the Press: An Analysis of Press Content in 1952 Senatorial Campaigns* (East Lansing: Governmental Research Bureau, Michigan State College, 1954), pp. 65-71.

25 James W. Markham, "Press Treatment of the 1958 State Elections in Pennsylvania," *Western Political Quarterly*, XIV (1961), 921.

26 James E. Gregg, "Newspaper Editorial Endorsements and California Elections, 1948-62," *Journalism Quarterly*, XLII (1965), 533.

27 Nathan B. Blumberg, *One-Party Press?* (Lincoln: University of Nebraska Press, 1954), pp. 44-5.

28 Guido H. Stempel III, "The Prestige Press Covers the 1960 Presidential Campaign," *Journalism Quarterly*, XXXVIII (1961), 157-163, and "The Prestige Press in Two Presidential Elections," *Journalism Quarterly*, XLII (1965), 15-21.

29 Jae-won Lee, "Editorial Support and Campaign News: Content Analysis by Q-Method," *Journalism Quarterly*, XLIX (Winter 1972), 715. For some delightful and insightful comments on the media in presidential campaigning see Timothy Crouse, *The Boys on the Bus* (New York: Random House, 1973).

30 Robert Batlin, "San Francisco Newspapers' Campaign Coverage: 1896-1952," *Journalism Quarterly*, XXXI (1954), 297-303.

31 Frank Luther Mott, "Newspapers in Presidential Campaigns," *Public Opinion Quarterly*, VIII (1944), 358.

32 A careful survey panel study of Milwaukee voters in 1968 concluded on this point that "media editorials — whether written or spoken — have relatively little influence on the *presidential* voting decision." — *The 1968 Campaign: Anatomy of A Crucial Election* (Washington, D.C.: The American Institute for Political Communication, 1970), p. 2; italics in original. On the other hand, the Survey Research Center of the University of Michigan recently reported that "in 1968 newspaper endorsements may have given Nixon the winning edge. . .[and] that newspaper endorsements have been consistently related to the presidential vote." — *ISR Newsletter*, I (Winter 1974), 3.

33 Gregg, *op. cit.*, pp. 534-6.

34 John E. Mueller, "Choosing Among 133 Candidates," *Public Opinion Quarterly*, XXXIV (1970), 400.

35 John P. Robinson, "Perceived Media Bias and the 1968 Vote: Can the Media Affect Behavior After All?" *Journalism Quarterly*, XLIX (Summer 1972), 245.

[36] Doris A. Graber, "Personal Qualities in Presidential Images: The Contribution of the Press," *Midwest Journal of Political Science*, XVI (February 1972), 71-2.

[37] Bernard C. Cohen, *The Public's Impact on Foreign Policy* (Boston: Little, Brown and Company, 1973), p. 178. See also Senator J. W. Fulbright, *The Pentagon Propaganda Machine* (New York: Liveright Publishing Corp., 1970).

[38] David L. Paletz, Peggy Reichert, and Barbara McIntyre, "How the Media Support Local Governmental Authority," *Public Opinion Quarterly*, XXXV (1971), 92.

[39] George Seldes, "The One-Party Press," *New York Times*, September 5, 1973. See also David Wise, *The Politics of Lying: Government Deception, Secrecy and Power* (New York: Random House, 1973).

[40] Reston says, on this point: "Congressmen are different. Unlike officials of the Executive, they live most of the time in the open. They think the good opinion of the press is important to their re-election, which interests them, so they see us and some of them even read us. Also, they are always making speeches and, like reporters, looking for mistakes to correct or criticize, especially if they are in the opposition. So the reporter and the Congressman are often natural allies." James Reston, *Sketches in the Sand* (New York: Alfred A. Knopf, Inc., 1967), p. 192.

[41] *New York Times*, November 1, 1962.

[42] Bill Moyers, "Read This, Please, But Don't Tell Anyone What It Says or Who Wrote It. If You Must Tell, Attribute It To A Former Government Aide Writing in a Large Metropolitan Daily," *New York Times*, January 6, 1972.

7 Opinions and Public Policy

Old opinions change, and new opinions are formed. But how? Under what circumstances, as a consequence of what forces, and with what political results? In this chapter I raise some questions about how these changes affect political life and public policy.

MODELS OF OPINION AND ATTITUDE CHANGE

As with so much else in modern psychology, Freud and his followers seem to have been the first psychological investigators to consider the possibilities — and to some extent the dynamics — of attitude change. Earlier, the study of psychology tended to be static, descriptive, and concerned with the nature of presumed "drives" such as egoism, or with the pleasure-pain formulation. From the beginning, psychoanalysis had both the advantage and the disadvantage of being developed in the context of therapy and medicine. Freud's methodology, though very unscientific in many ways, had an empirical base; he dealt with real people who had real psychological problems. And, more important for the point being made here, his objective was to produce changes in attitudes and attitude structures (and in even deeper levels of the personality.)

Unfortunately, the Freudian concern for attitude change is too limited and too narrow to meet the demands for generalization made in this book. The very features that moved the Freudians to concern themselves with attitude change — namely, a desire to reduce neurotic and psychotic conflicts in the individual — were also those that now limit the usefulness of Freudian conceptualization for the general study of attitude change.

There are two other and more general approaches to the study of opinion change: (a) *balance theory* and (b) *functional theory*. I will briefly describe each; but the systematic statement of attitude change that follows the descriptions is in terms of a functional analysis that incorporates balance mechanisms.

Balance theory[1] is based on the proposition that the human organism needs and seeks a total configuration of beliefs, attitudes, and behavior that reflects (a) internal consistency, (b) a general state of equilibrium, and (c) the objective facts of the environment. Not all beliefs, attitudes, and behavior need to be regarded as rational, but rationality plays an important part in balance theory. The belief structure that is in equilibrium will reflect reason as well as irrational needs, the individual's state of knowledge or of ignorance, and a host of environmental factors of which cultural prescriptions and group pressures are among the most important.

If major perceived inconsistencies exist between the cognitive and affective aspects of an attitude, or between different attitudes, balance theory would predict some direct or indirect changes to bring the attitude or attitudes into greater consistency. The basic, generalized proposition of the balance theory of attitude change has been stated as follows:

When the affective and cognitive components of an attitude are mutually consistent, the attitude is in a stable state; when the affective and cognitive components are mutually inconsistent (to a degree that exceeds the individual's present tolerance for such inconsistency), the attitude is in an unstable state and will undergo spontaneous reorganizing activity until such activity eventuates in either (1) the attainment of affective-cognitive consistency or (2) the placing of an "irreconcilable" inconsistency beyond the range of active awareness.[2]

The third, most general, and most integrating approach to the study of attitude dynamics is the *functional approach.* "The basic assumption . . . is that both attitude formation and attitude change must be understood in terms of the needs they serve and that as these motivational processes differ, so too will the conditions and techniques for attitude change."[3]

Katz has categorized the four major functions of attitudes as:

1. *The instrumental, adjustive, or utilitarian function:* "Essentially, this function is a recognition of the fact that people strive to maximize the rewards in their external environment and to minimize the penalties. . . .the dynamics of attitude formation with respect to the adjustment function are dependent upon present or post perceptions of the utility of the attitudinal object for the individual."

2. *The knowledge function:* People, Katz says, "seek knowledge to give meaning to what would otherwise be an unorganized chaotic universe. People need standards or frames of reference for understanding their world, and attitudes help to supply such standards" by providing definiteness, distinction, consistency, and stability. The difference between the utilitarian and knowledge functions is that attitudes serving the utilitarian function tell us what we need to believe to get along with the social world, while attitudes serving the knowledge function tell us what is accurate or true about our environment. Thus the knowledge function is a special case of the utilitarian, with heavy (but not exclusive) emphasis on cognitive elements.

3. *The value-expressive function:* These attitudes give "positive expression to [the individual's] central values and to the type of person he conceives himself to be." Such attitudes are in a sense the reciprocal of the ego-defensive attitudes; ego-defensive attitudes are designed to prevent damage to the self-image, whereas value-expressive attitudes enhance the self-image.

4. *The ego-defensive function:* The individual "protects himself from acknowledging the basic truths about himself or the harsh realities in his external world." Devices by which the individual defends his ego (his self-image) include those

designed to avoid the dissonant elements entirely – denial, misinterpretation – and those, less incapacitating, which distort, the dissonant elements – rationalization, projection, displacement.[4]

Although a great deal (perhaps most) of the attention given to attitudes and attitude change has been directed at understanding the way that attitudes contribute to the ego-defensive and value-expressive functions, it is likely that the utilitarian and knowledge functions are more important for the everyday life of the individual. This proposition is, doubtless, especially true for the *political* attitudes of the average American; the evidence is overwhelming that politics are not ego-related for most people – although we must bear in mind the relevance of *role* and *elite* factors. Most people do not construe public issues as capable of threatening or enhancing the self-image. The average citizen does not internalize political ideologies or controversies to the point where they matter at any other than the most superficial levels of consciousness. For political leaders, however, quite the reverse may be true; the ego-defensive and value-expressive functions may become so important that their satisfaction impedes the knowledge and utilitarian functions.

Let me try to put all the above together in one summary sentence. *The process of opinion change, from the point of view of functional analysis, appears to operate as follows:*

The individual becomes aware of (perceives), ordinarily at the conscious level, a new stimulus (a message, in communication terms); IF

(a) the stimulus is seen as related to attitudes serving one or more of the functions named above, and

(b) the stimulus is internalized (cognitively or affectively or both) in such a way that imbalance is created in an existing attitude or attitudes, and

(c) the imbalance is sufficiently disruptive, THEN

(d) cognitive or affective (or both) aspects of the existing attitude or attitudes will be changed until the imbalance is reduced.

It is clear from this statement of the process that opinion change will take place only if a number of conditions are met. Attitudes and opinions are remarkably stable – and necessarily so, for maintenance of the individual's mental health and for dependability in social interaction.

Resistance to attitude change is ordinarily high; habit and stereotypical thinking satisfy most of the functional needs of most people; and messages may be quite easily distorted to fit into existing attitudes, thus eliminating the need for change.

OPINION AND BEHAVIOR: CONSISTENCY AND CHANGE

People do not always say what they think. People do not always act as they believe. Difficult as it is to discover attitudes and opinions, it is even more difficult to know when behavior reflects attitudes and opinions. We are not concerned with the problems of sources, development, or measurement of attitudes, or even whether opinions are consistent with attitudes. Here we are raising questions concerning the possibility that attitudes and opinions, under some circumstances, may be quite inconsistent with behavior.

Opinion-behavior inconsistencies are a common fact of life. I may dislike getting out of bed in the morning to go to work; yet I do it. I may loathe one of my colleagues; yet I act decently and perhaps even pleasantly toward him. I may be bored completely at a party; yet I laugh and talk and appear to the hostess to be enjoying myself immensely. As Shakespeare says, "one may smile, and smile, and be a villian."

There are several reasons why people may say what they do not believe:

1. They do not know what they believe and feel required to say something (we have already considered this matter, in part, under the "don't know" problem in Chapter 3).
2. They are unable to express what they believe (that is, their ability with language is too limited to express their opinions accurately).
3. They are unwilling to say what they believe.
4. They feel social pressure to tell a lie, believing the lie to be innocent, or that they will not be exposed.[5]

There is, no doubt, a tendency to consistency in the three elements of the complex involving (a) private opinions, (b) verbal expressions, (c) overt behavior. John Dollard believes that opinions, when voiced either spontaneously or in answer to queries, are expressions of "antici-patory" or "forecasting responses" — that is, they give clues to what the respondent believes he would do when faced with choices involving the substance of the question. The clearest political illustration is the answer to the question "Which candidate do you favor?" for the ques-tion implies the behavior component; namely, in whose behalf do you intend to act (vote)? Though the opinion poll of candidate preference is the most obvious example of the argument that voiced opinions are anticipatory responses, most survey answers can be thought of as fore-casts of behavior; questions about political ideology, policy issues, or political actors may be considered questions about what the respondent would *do* if choices were necessary. If one thinks about the problem in this way, as Dollard suggests, the question of consistency between opin-ion and behavior becomes one of how well the individual can predict his future behavior at the time that he has to make a statement about it (that is, at the time he expresses his opinion). Dollard makes some useful and unsophisticated generalizations about the psychological and sociological conditions under which opinions and behavior will be consistent:

1. Neurotics will find it difficult to predict their behavior when their own serious conflicts are involved.
2. Persons with poor verbal skills may find it difficult to forecast their own behavior.
3. People who habitually go into effective action after thinking things over can best predict their own actions.
4. The test situation should not be corrupted by extraneous threats or rewards.
5. A man can best predict what he will do in a future situation if he has been in about the same situation before and thus knows what it's all about.
6. A man can predict what he will do in a future situation provided he doesn't have an experience which changes his mind before this situation occurs.
7. A man can better predict what he will do in a future dilemma if he is told exactly what this dilemma will be.[6]

It should not be thought that behavior changes follow chronologi-cally, any more than logically, after opinion change. In many instances, opinions change, if at all, only *after* related behavior changes. As Berelson and Steiner point out:

> Behavior, being visible, is more responsive to extreme pressures and accommodations. OABs [opinions, attitudes, and beliefs], being private until expressed, can be maintained without even being subject to question or argument. And there is no necessary reason for OABs and behavior to be in harmony.[7]

Opinion change is apt to follow behavior change if the behavior is repeated, if it is approved by one's reference groups, and if it is sanctioned by the social environment generally. Under extreme conditions of deprivation, psychological, physical, or both, when support for pre-existing opinion is removed and contrary behavior is forced or strongly urged, very large shifts in attitudes and opinions may occur. The identification of Jewish concentration camp victims with their captors and the defection of American soldiers to communist "brainwashing" are celebrated examples of such extreme opinion shift following, or concurrent with, behavior changes.[8]

OPINION CHANGE AMONG POLITICAL ELITES

Opinion leaders, more than opinion followers or "ordinary citizens," are apt to have attitudes and opinions that are stable and resistant to change. Political leaders are shown to care more intensely about the ends and means of public policy and to hold their opinions more firmly, with greater articulateness and self-consciousness, and with greater persistence.[9] Given these anchorages to reality, and to their own personality and social needs, it is not surprising that the opinions of political leaders are least susceptible to whim and to the chance effects of random information or propaganda stimulation.

On the other hand, precisely because the views of opinion leaders are tied to reality and are more self-consciously held than those of the followers, significant changes in the environment of such leaders are apt to be evaluated more accurately and quickly by them, and are thus more apt to lead to appropriate changes. Rationality is more apt to characterize the opinion-change processes of opinion leaders. The collection and evaluation of relevant information, along with increased use of discussion and consultative devices, are likely to accompany opinion changes among social and political elites. Theoretical models that emphasize cognitive balance will be more useful in the explanation of elite opinion change then they will be in the explanation of nonelite change. In sum, among political leaders (by contrast with nonleaders), opinion change is apt to be less volatile, more deliberate, more informed by social fact and trends, and more predictable; and at the same time (in a free society), more gradual and incremental in its pace and scope.[10]

NON-ELITE OPINION CHANGE

For most people political questions are not important. Politics and public issues play only small and episodic parts in the lives of most individuals. This low salience has great significance for opinion-behavior consistency and inconsistency. If people have little motivation, little knowledge, and few occasions to experience relevant stimuli, they will display a great range of attitudes, opinions, and verbal behavior, often logically and politically inconsistent.

Two or more expressed opinions given casually and in an offhand manner by a person who has little interest in the subject probably will be independent of each other, and may be logically inconsistent. Such opinions may be related in some loose way to larger, more general, attitudes; but unless these relationships become recognized by the individual, no inconsistencies will be felt and there will be no tendencies to bring the disparate opinions together for comparison or change to greater consistency. If, later, the same question is answered a different way, this does not mean that change has occurred, but merely that the earlier question and answer, being unimportant, were not remembered. In such cases analytical theories like Festinger's notions of cognitive dissonance are inappropriate; only when attitudes and opinions are important to him will the individual care whether they are consistent with one another.

When giving their opinions, people have both internal and external reasons for consistency or inconsistency. When a person has high internal motivation and high interest, opinions are most apt to be consistent and change is least apt to occur. This is the general case of the opinion elites. If, in addition to high internal motivation and interest, there is strong environmental support for consistent opinions, and if the community is seen to regard the issue as a matter of importance, then there will be the highest consistency and least change of opinion over time.

Conversely, when persons have little internal motivation and interest, and when the environment is seen as being both unsupportive and uninterested, then there will be greater inconsistency and most apparent change over time. This is the general case of the apathetic person who, instead of giving the more honest answer of "don't know" or "don't care," gives casual answers to questions about public issues.

Among the several practical applications of this way of conceptualizing opinion and behavior consistency is the meaning it gives to political campaigns. Campaigns increase the environmental motivations, making issues and political opinions temporarily more salient and allowing persons whose opinions and behavior are idiosyncratically inconsistent to learn what the "party line" and what majority or peer-group sentiment may be, or to ponder the issues more carefully, and thus to increase consistency, rationality, and predictable behavior.

OPINION CHANGE AND POLICY CHANGE

Opinions matter for policy. The reason is simple: Opinions are usually reflected in votes; and, in a democracy, votes — if ever so indirectly — make policy.

Whatever science there is in government is the science of probabilities — of the probabilities that those who participate in government, however much or little, from the president to the once-in-a-lifetime voter, will behave in predictable ways. All analyses of political relationships rest on such probabilities. For policies and administrative ways that are long settled, and to which the power network of the society is well adjusted, the probabilities of predictable behavior are very high. In the 1970s support for the United States social-security system is very high, and policymakers in Washington can rely on the routine compliance of 99 percent or more of those involved. In the middle 1930s that was not the case; the opinions of those involved were then so sharply polarized that the probability of obtaining agreement was perhaps no greater than 60 percent.

Perhaps one can generalize the interdependence of opinions and the political process as public policies evolve from private thoughts. Earlier we described the opinion-policy process; that was a description of political sociology based on the group theory of politics, and it was somewhat static in that no account was taken of changes in numbers, intensities, or salience of individual or group opinions. The scheme offered here has different components, although it interlocks with the earlier presentation in many ways, most of which are obvious.

Public policies evolve from governmental responses to human needs and desires. All public policies were once merely *private ideas*. Private ideas, when shared by large numbers of individuals, become *proposals*. Proposals, when they are adopted by governmental authorities, become *public policies*. So simplified, these three stages are clear, although it must be at once obvious that, while the distinction between a proposal and a public policy is marked by an official act (by an executive signature or a legislative engrossment) and by a point of time (the "effective date"), no such sharp distinction can be made between an idea and a proposal. The simplified trichotomy is thus:

Idea (private) ⎯⎯⎯⎯▶ Proposal ⎯⎯⎯⎯▶ Policy (public)

Immediately we elaborate. More extreme than ideas are unthinkable thoughts — which may be called *latent ideas*, but which are proscribed by the culture and will be given the name of *sacrilege*. Beyond policy is *tradition*, which may be called *assimilated policies*, and which is required by culture (just as sacrilege is forbidden by culture). As we noted earlier, in modern societies very little is forbidden to ideas; sacrilege is almost an extinct commodity in the Western world, and it is rapidly disappearing in non-Western lands. On the other hand, considerable tradition, in its post- or ultrapolicy form, exists. The English common law is perhaps the best example of the dynamic relationship between tradition and policy. The body of practices from which the common law is drawn is precisely a tradition about which there is so much agreement that conflict seldom arises. When conflict does arise over this tradition, a policy statement — that is, a judicial application of the common law — has to be made to settle it; but it can hardly be denied, if one accepts the common-law system at all, that such a tradition is ordinarily beyond contention. With sacrilege and tradition added, the schema becomes:

[Sacrilege] ◀⎯⎯▶ Idea ⎯⎯⎯▶ Proposal ⎯⎯⎯▶ Policy ◀⎯⎯▶ [Tradition]
                  (private)   (public)

Let us add a simple representation of opinion, not to take account of the rich variety of views that flower in the attentive public at the proposal stage, but simply to represent the probability of agreement. Thus:

[Sacrilege] ◄───► Idea ───► Proposal ───► Policy ◄───► [Tradition]

0% ─── 100%

Probability of agreement

Greater detail and concern for realism will move us to represent some of the characteristics of the proposal stage. Between idea and proposal come agitation, education, and diffusion of the idea. Organization and politicization follow or come about concurrently as the numbers of supporters (and, very likely, opponents, too) grow and as the intensity of opinions increases. At some point public notice is taken of the *idea-become-proposal*, and governmental officials move for its transformation into policy. In this way the proposal takes the form of a motion, a resolution, a bill, or an executive order. Intensification of opinions and nongovernmental-organization efforts proceed rapidly at this stage, and at some time a decision is made to stop the proposal (temporarily or permanently, as time will reveal) or to move it to the policy stage:

Education   ⎫ ⎧ Public action: ⎫ │ Law followed by appeal and
Organization   ⎬ ⎨ bill, resolution,   ⎬ │ uncertainty, then routinization
Politicization   ⎭ ⎩ executive order   ⎭ │

[Sacrilege] ◄───► Idea ───► Proposal ───► Policy ◄─── [Tradition]

0% ─── 100%

Probability of agreement

One other element needs to be added to our schema: a representation of numbers and intensities of opinions. As the proposal stage moves to a climax, the general case will exhibit a maximization of involvement, both mass and elite, of intensity and notoriety. In short, more people will care more about the proposal (keeping in mind that even *more* people may not be a large percentage of the population). After the decision is made to end it at the proposal stage or to move it on to the policy stage, both intensity and notoriety fall off. If the proposal fails to become policy, its supporters lose some interest, out of discouragement and rationalization, and its opponents withdraw somewhat from the battle. If the proposal becomes policy, its supporters tend to rest on their laurels and its opponents suffer the fait accompli effect — namely, the withdrawal of emotional attachment and a rationalization of the changed state of affairs on the part of the losers. Size of the interested public, and the intensities of opinions, may be represented by the crosshatch area in the completed schema below.[11]

The political salience of an issue is the amount of political heat generated by the issue, a measure of its importance, and a composite of numbers and intensities of opinions.

Two points should be made about the schema — although both are quite obvious. The first is that in any given case history of policy development great distortions from the model may appear. The idea-to-proposal-to-policy stages may be completed before there is sufficient politicization and political salience to ensure a high enough probability of agreement

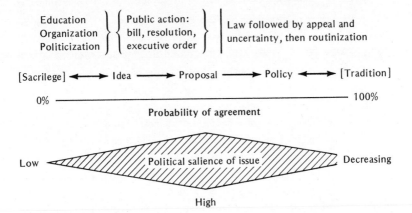

— this is what happened in the case of the hurried, unpopular, and unenforceable Eighteenth Amendment. Conversely, the probability of agreement on an issue may be very high, but because of a volatile and episodic political salience or because of institutional advantages enjoyed by minorities, the proposal may never become policy: Compulsory military training is a case in point; perhaps even a better example is the proposal for a conflict-of-interest law that would apply to Congress, which would command widespread popular support but which has been avoided by a Congress understandably reluctant to limit its own freedom. The second point is that the schema has no necessary time schedule built into it. The whole process may be very quickly experienced, as was the case with the creation of a federal policy toward the making and the use of nuclear energy.[12] On the other hand, decades, even centuries may elapse in the evolution of a proposal from an idea.

The schema illustrates why existing policy (the status quo) has the advantage over proposals. Once acceptance for policy has become widespread and salience has decreased, the probability of agreement rises while the level of importance goes down. Real or imagined advantages may be found in the policy, and, as lives are adjusted to the demands and benefits of the policy, support for it increases. Or, at the very least, attention is reduced by the adoption of a better-the-known-evil perspective. At an even higher level of generalization there is a presumption in favor of existing policy, a presumption compounded of the ease of the habit principle, the majesty of the law, and desire for social stability, which can be achieved only when there is much agreement on many governmental policies.

The conceptualization above is, quite obviously, still incomplete as an explanation of the way an idea becomes public policy through a "natural history" involving the spread of the idea, the mobilization of support, the debate about alternatives, and the legislation of the idea as policy into governmental routines. Still missing is a generalization about the political process by which the proposal becomes law in the context of the official and unofficial machinery of a representative democracy. We have not shown how the dynamics of increased political salience and increased probability of agreement are related to the institutional dynamics of policy change. We have not accounted for the role of governmental agencies (legislatures, executives, bureaucracies, and courts), or for the roles of parties and pressure groups. To do so, even in a preliminary and inadequate way, we may recall our conceptualization of the opinion-policy process.

The original model of this opinion-policy process was limited to the interactions of expressed opinions, through group memberships and alignments, on legislative action. Majority, minority, and effective opinions were differentiated and some consideration was given to the way group memberships mediate the opinions of individuals so that the language of politics speaks of "carrying the farm vote," "alienating labor," or "losing favor in the business community." The initial model of the opinion-policy process frankly adopted the point of view that has become known as the *group theory of politics* – a point of view that, however inadequate it may be for the nuances of political explanation and prediction, represents what I regard to be the most useful basic orientation to the study of American politics. Bearing that model in mind, let's see if we can describe (and show in Fig. 7-1) how changes in individual opinions, changes in opinion distribution, and changes in levels of politicization operate through political groups and governmental institutions to bring about policy change.

Opinion change in the individual is related to policy change in the government by linkages that transmit new or revised opinions, usually through the mediation of groups, to policymakers in such form and intensity that the policymakers are moved to change policy. A representation of individual opinion-change processes, social policy-change processes, and their linkages through elections and groups is shown in Figure 7-1. It is unnecessary to repeat here the details of the opinion-change processes, at the individual level, as described in an earlier section of this book. Elites are distinguished from nonelites by levels of knowledge of, interest in, and participation in public affairs. The collective evidence from field and experimental studies indicates that opinion-change for elites (as compared with nonelites) will involve (a) the more accurate perception of stimuli relevant to the issue about which the opinion has been or is to be formed; (b) more detailed cognitive structuring and interpretation of the source and form of the stimuli; (c) more complex and realistic manipulation of the stimuli meanings in terms of personality and environmental factors; (d) greater recognition of the fact of change (i.e., crossing the threshold for response when and if it occurs); and, finally, (e) more complex and multiple use of the response factors (i.e., adjustment, denial, conversion, displacement, and rationalization).[13]

In Figure 7-1 the arrows connecting elites and nonelites are meant to represent two conditions. The first is that democracy supposes, and American society in large measure provides for, free and relatively easy transition from one status to the other. Simply by increasing her knowledge, interest, and participation in political affairs a person may move from nonelite to elite — bearing in mind, of course, that such changes are not "simply" made, but are almost always aspects of complicated and fundamental changes in education, socioeconomic conditions, life styles, and personality. The second point represented by the connecting arrows between elites and nonelites has to do, actually, with the social rather than the individual level of analysis, but it could not be shown

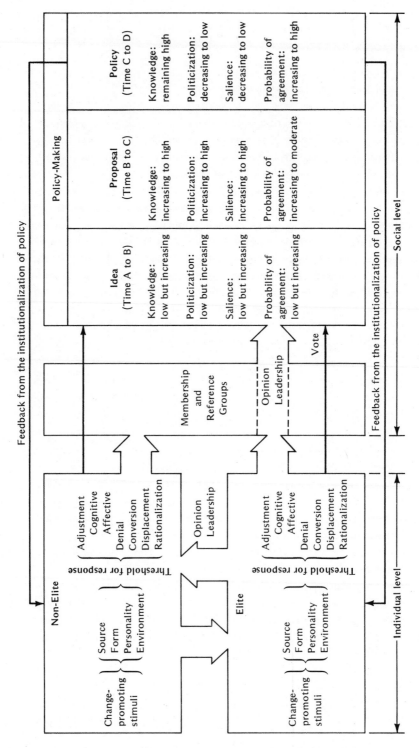

FIGURE 7-1. Opinion Change and Policy Change

otherwise in the figure. It is that the opinion changes of each group influence the opinion-change processes of the other group. The nonelite find easier acquiescence in their own opinion changes if testimonials from the elite support their new opinions; the elite are strengthened both in their opinion changes and in their general elite status if their opinions find ready acceptance among members of the nonelite.

Both elites and nonelites form, test, and revise their opinions, in a dynamic and never-ending series of choices, in large part by referring to groups that are important. Reference groups, those that are regarded by the individual as providing standards for the appropriateness or inappropriateness of opinions and attitudes, are more important than membership groups for the individual processes of opinion change. But – *and note this well* – in making the linkage from individual opinions to public policy the policymaker must rely heavily on the size and activity of membership groups. The reference group is a psychological fiction, a construct that helps us understand why people hold the attitudes and opinions they do, but it is not a concept or condition that can be aggregated directly for political purposes. The membership group, however, is ideally suited to policy manipulation, coalition-building, and rationalization.

The obvious and immediate advantage, for political life, of the membership group over the reference group has two important consequences. First, it introduces considerable distortion of the true distribution of opinion. The policymaker assumes that individuals employ as reference groups these groups of which they are members. Of course, there is an automatic discount made in the minds of policymakers, but the tendency is for them to believe that veterans' organizations can speak for veterans or medical societies can speak for doctors (i.e., that veterans use veterans' organizations as reference groups on certain issues, and that doctors use medical societies as reference groups on some issues). Such a presumption is, undoubtedly, in a rough and ready way, valid for political analysis and strategy; but real opinions get distorted. The second consequence of the political importance of membership groups is that group officials and spokesmen become key communication channels between private individuals and policymakers. Opinion leadership becomes, then, a function not merely of elite criteria (i.e., knowledge, interest, and participation), but also of position and status as recognized official or spokesman for a recognized group.

The lines labeled "vote," running from elites and nonelites through groups to policymaking, are meant to represent more than the mere act of voting. They symbolize the linkages through the electoral processes that, on the one hand, represent the only *direct* influence the individual can have on choosing policymakers, and, on the other hand, are strongly influenced and mediated by group attachments. One way of putting it is to say that opinions about candidates (and referenda issues), while formed as are other opinions internally and through reference to groups, have the additional and direct channel of expression via the ballot. It is the particular task of the political parties, as one kind of membership and reference group, to influence the vote. The political interest group (any group that seeks to serve as a reference group for individuals with regard to opinions about the objectives of the group) may also focus on the vote — but will, more than political parties, diffuse its energies throughout all the processes shown in Figure 7-1 in pursuit of its specialized policy objectives.

The large box labeled "Policymaking" is a representation of the way opinions are funded, interpreted, and given meaning as policies are arrived at through legislation, executive action, and judicial action. It shows the relative changes to be expected in levels of knowledge, politicization, salience, and probability of agreement as issues move from the idea stage to the proposal stage to the policy stage.

I assume that policymakers, as individuals, are subject to the same kinds of opinion-change processes as other members of the political elite, and that each individually interacts with other policymakers, as is indicated in Figure 7-1. For the policymakers collectively I also assume an equilibrium model in which no change is expected unless the pro-change pressures felt by the policymakers are greater (by some quantity we can call system threshold for change) than the antichange pressures felt by them. The elements of pro- or antichange pressures are both internal and external. Internal pressures refer to personal attitudes and opinions of policymakers, reflecting their ideologies, personality needs, and their level of knowledge about the issue. External pressures are those arising from the social institutions, group identifications, and communications networks that impinge on the policymakers, and are seen by them to be relevant to the issue under consideration.

In practice, internal and external pressures are systematically related. While the ideologies and personality needs of policymakers presumably change slowly, their opinions and votes on proposals may change suddenly from an increase in level of knowledge, resulting from such external factors as interest-group activities or access to a communication channel previously closed. Moreover, the relationship between external pressures and internal pressures is not one-way. The common conception of pluralistic politics is that interest groups put pressure on policymakers, but just as often it seems that policymakers actively seek the pressure of interest groups, and also place the interest groups under countervailing pressure and constraints. Policymakers look for interpretation and facts that will strengthen positions they intend, for prior reasons, to support.

Finally, the arrows from "Policy" back to the individuals represent the effects on individuals of the establishment of new or revised policy and the institutionalization of that policy into programs and bureaucratic procedures. As new or changed policy is implemented by field programs and central bureaucratization, differential effects on taxation and/or service levels will be felt by various individuals and groups. These changes may then be perceived as new change-producing stimuli bringing about new imbalance and resulting in further individual responses (adjustment, denial, etc.) and revisions of individual-group and group-group relations.

In response to changes in the opinion environment, policymakers will make adjustments in their own thinking and behavior. Some of these adjustments will be of a regularized and bureaucratic nature — change-promoting forces may have to follow prescribed forms of petition, bill-drafting, and orderly progression from district to central officials; and change-resisting forces will have the same or other channels of institutionalized access or influence.

Beyond the general constraints of bureaucracy, there are other sets of variables that have significance for the processes by which opinions are translated into public policy. First, the influence of opinion in policymaking will vary with the specific organizational context within which the decisionmakers operate. If the governmental agencies have elaborate and specialized services for collecting and processing information about public opinion, they are likely to pay more attention to the distribution of popular and group views on the issues at stake. Governmental agencies obviously vary in the extent to which they are able and willing to provide such facilities for collecting and analyzing opinion distributions. Historically, among United States federal agencies, the State Department and the Agriculture Department have provided more of such services for policymakers than have such departments as Interior and Defense. Most governmental agencies at state and local levels make little or no effort to provide decisionmakers with systematic intelligence on the distribution of opinions.[14]

Second, the time demands of the decision situation will have important consequences for the opinion-policy process. If the situation is regarded as one of crisis, there will be little time to measure and weigh the opinion distributions on the matter at hand. A crisis situation is one in which there is a short period of time in which to respond to a basic threat that was not anticipated by the decisionmakers. Under such circumstances, public opinion will be less important in the decision. The development of United States atomic-energy policy in 1945-46 is a case in point. The 1961 decision to block Soviet expansion in Cuba was another case in which public opinion was less influential than it was in, say, the 1948 decision to provide massive aid to European countries through the Marshall Plan.

Finally, the impact of opinions will vary with the personality characteristics of the decisionmakers. Some political leaders are inclined to attach less importance to public opinion – or, if they grant its importance in the policymaking processes, to show great confidence in their abilities to judge it for themselves. Thus, Woodrow Wilson was not disposed to accept advice on either the importance or the status of popular or group opinions on the issues with which he was confronted as president. Presidents Kennedy, Johnson, and Nixon, on the other hand, seemed much more inclined to pay attention to polls, newspaper reports, and professionals who were reputed to have their "ears to the ground." Thus, these factors, internal to the official government – generalized bureaucratic routinization, specialized services for reporting and assessing public opinion, crisis level of the decision situation, and personality differences of decisionmakers – must all be considered in the elaborated model of the opinion-policy process.

Political parties enter the opinion-policy process in two ways: first, in their efforts to determine who the officeholders will be in the official government; and, second, in their efforts to mediate and compromise the conflicts among interest groups. American political parties are primarily interested in winning public office. To win public office under two-party conditions, a candidate must normally receive a clear majority of the vote. To win a clear majority of the votes, a candidate must attract from individuals and groups greater support than his opponent attracts. The art of politics consists, then, in gaining and keeping a coalition of support greater than an opponent's coalition of support.

Politicians and political parties are thus the policy brokers of the American democracy — softening, mediating, and reconciling the inter-group conflict, and, at the same time, "peopling" the government with legislators, executives, judges, and administrators, whose function it is to make and carry out policies that are tolerable for most groups, if perfect for none.

The above description of the function of parties is familiar to all. To represent this in Figure 7-1 is a difficult matter, however, because the political party embraces all the elements shown in that figure. The parties bind individuals and groups together with the official govern-ment; the party apparatuses within the governments provide organiza-tion and procedures for the processes by which proposals become transformed into policy; and the parties, through their mass organizations and the communications media, provide a vital element in the feedback channels that are so important for opinion stability and opinion change. The parties — to use an organic analogy, dangerous as they can be — are like the lymphatic system of the human body, not separable and discrete like the lungs or heart but generally infused throughout the whole organ-ism. Like the lymphatic system, the parties inform and sustain the body politic, sometimes highlighting differences but more often compromising conflict, searching out and supporting leaders and spokesmen who are representative, and providing channels for all who care about the con-tinuation of the democratic dialogue.

In the end, however, even this more elaborate representation of the opinion-policy process, including the overlay of the party system; like all such schemata, is much too simple and anemic to catch the richness of complex human and governmental processes. For any adequate under-standing of the dynamics of opinion and policy change, one must envi-sion the varied involvement of thousands of groups and potential groups, and of tens or hundreds of thousands of individuals, some caring a lot and others not much, some with skills and resources at their command and others with little — all initiating, responding, evaluating, calculating, and projecting their strategies toward the reduction of their grievances and the enhancement of their happiness. Such is the process of government where individuals are free to form, hold, and revise their opinions, where their opinions may be openly expressed and related to behavior, and where social institutions encourage such opinion-holding individuals to participate — as their inclinations and abilities permit — in the public enterprise.

Notes:

[1] I have adopted the term *balance* because I believe that the words "consistency" and "inconsistency" have some logical and evaluative connotations that social science should avoid as much as possible. I would use Festinger's term "dissonance," but I do not find his formulation the most useful for students of public opinion and the opinion-policy process. Festinger's major statement provides inadequate attention to the affective elements of individual attitudes and to the nonrational capacities and devices to tolerate rational inconsistencies. See Leon Festinger, *A Theory of Cognitive Dissonance* (New York: Harper & Row, Inc., 1957). For a critical review of the work of Festinger and his students, see Natalia P. Chapanis and Alphonse Chapanis, "Cognitive Dissonance: Five Years Later," *Psychological Bulletin*, LXI (1964), 1-22.

[2] Milton J. Rosenberg, "An Analysis of Affective-Cognitive Consistency," in Rosenberg *et al.*, eds., *Attitude Organization and Change* (New Haven, Conn.: Yale University Press, 1960), p. 22.

[3] Daniel Katz, "The Functional Approach to the Study of Attitudes," *Public Opinion Quarterly*, XXIV (1960), 167. For much of what follows I am indebted to this thoughtful and illuminating essay by Katz. Quotations reprinted by permission.

[4] *Ibid.*, 170-5.

[5] A common source of misrepresentation (lying), referred to in an earlier chapter, is pressure to appear to be a good citizen. Opinion surveys consistently show that 30 to 40 percent of Americans say they would make a small contribution to their political parties; however, very little door-to-door partisan fund-raising has been judged to be worth the effort — *Electing Congress: The Financial Dilemma*, Report of the Task Force on Financing Congressional Campaigns (New York: Twentieth Century Fund, 1970), pp. 62-5.

[6] John Dollard, "Under What Conditions Do Opinions Predict Behavior?" *Public Opinion Quarterly*, XII (1948-49), 628-32. See also Robert Audi, "On the Conception and Measurement of Attitudes in Contemporary Anglo-American Psychology," *Journal for the Theory of Social Behavior*, II (October 1972), 179-203, especially p. 192ff.

[7] Bernard Berelson and Gary A. Steiner, *Human Behavior: An Inventory of Scientific Findings* (New York: Harcourt, Brace & World, Inc., 1964), p. 576. For discussion of the interrelations and dynamics of

behavioral change without related attitude change, see also Milton Rokeach, *Beliefs, Attitudes and Values: A Theory of Organization and Change* (San Francisco: Jossey-Bass, Inc., 1968), pp. 142-7.

[8] The Jews who identified with their Nazi guards and the soldiers who "confessed" and defected to the communists were few and were extremely deviant cases; see Bruno Bettelheim, "Individual and Mass Behavior in Extreme Situations," in Eleanor E. Maccoby *et al., Readings in Social Psychology* (New York: Holt, Rinehart and Winston, Inc., 1958), pp. 300-10; and, for a balanced assessment of the practices of communist brainwashers, see Albert D. Biderman, "The Image of 'Brainwashing,'" *Public Opinion Quarterly*, XXVI (1962), 547-63.

[9] Herbert McClosky, Paul J. Hoffman, and Rosemary O'Hara, "Issue Conflict and Consensus among Party Leaders and Followers," *American Political Science Review*, LIV (1960), 406-27; Robert S. Hirschfield, Bert E. Swanson, and Blanche D. Blank, "A Profile of Political Activists in Manhattan," *The Western Political Quarterly*, XV (1962), 489-506; Herbert McClosky, "Consensus and Ideology in American Politics," *American Political Science Review*, LVIII (1964), 361-82; and John H. Kessel, "Cognitive Dimensions and Political Activity," *Public Opinion Quarterly*, XXXIX (1965), 377-89.

[10] See Philip E. Converse, "The Nature of Belief Systems in Mass Publics," in David Apter, ed., *Ideology and Discontent* (New York: The Free Press, 1965), 206-61; Norman R. Luttbeg, "The Structure of Beliefs among Leaders and the Public," *Public Opinion Quarterly*, XXXII (1968), 398-409; David E. RePass, "Issue Salience and Party Choice," *American Political Science Review*, LXV (June 1971), 389-400; and Stephen Earl Bennett, "Consistency Among the Public's Social Welfare Policy Attitudes in the 1960s," *American Journal of Political Science*, XVII (August 1973), 544-70.

[11] For an overall view of the public policymaking process in America, see Charles O. Jones, *An Introduction to the Study of Public Policy* (Belmont, Calif.: Wadsworth Publishing Co., Inc., 1970).

[12] See Harold P. Green and Alan Rosenthal, *Government of the Atom* (New York: Atherton Press, 1963), pp. 1-5.

[13] It is tempting also to believe that elites employ greater reason and logic in their opinion-change processes — and there seems to be some evidence for believing they do, although this happy conclusion may be largely a result of pro-logic biases in the research designs and wishful thinking of investigators.

[14] For the points made in this and the next two paragraphs, I am indebted to James A. Robinson; see his statement of them in James A. Robinson and Richard C. Snyder, "Decision-Making in International Politics," in Herbert C. Kelman, ed., *International Behavior: A Social Psychological Analysis* (New York: Holt, Rinehart and Winston, 1965), pp. 435-63, especially pp. 456-8.

Index